FAMILY FLIP QUIZ

and the ha
find it the
on what y

KEY TO SYMB

- Science &
- The Arts
- People in History
- Exploration & Discovery
- Warfare & Weapons

You will find over 2000 questions here on the people and events through history. This is how to use your Flip Quiz: if you are answering questions on your own just cover the answers with your hand or a piece of card. You may want to write down your answers and count up your scores for each quiz.

If you are doing the quizzes with a partner or in teams, unfold the base and stand the Flip Quiz on a flat surface between you and your partner. Read aloud the questions (but not the answers!) and allow your partner to say the answers or write them down. You may answer each question in turn or answer an entire quiz in turn. Keep your scores on a piece of paper and compare results.

The illustrations are there to help you get the right answers when competing with a partner. For instance, if you are answering Quiz 1 questions, you will be looking at and reading out Quiz 2. However, the illustrations you will see are clues to help you do Quiz 1. Look at the labels by the illustrations. These tell you which question they are clues for. The pictures behind the quiz numbers at the top of the page are not such obvious clues, but they may still help you get the answer.

The questions are divided into six subjects: General Knowledge, Warfare and Weapons, People in History, Science and Technology, Exploration and Discovery, The Arts. You should attempt all questions though.

As you progress through the quizzes you will notice that the questions get a little harder. We think the easiest level is level 1

Levels
There are three levels of question – they get harder as you progress

Question categories
The questions are divided into six subjects (see key above)

Picture clues 1
These visual clues are not always obvious (and they don't have labels)

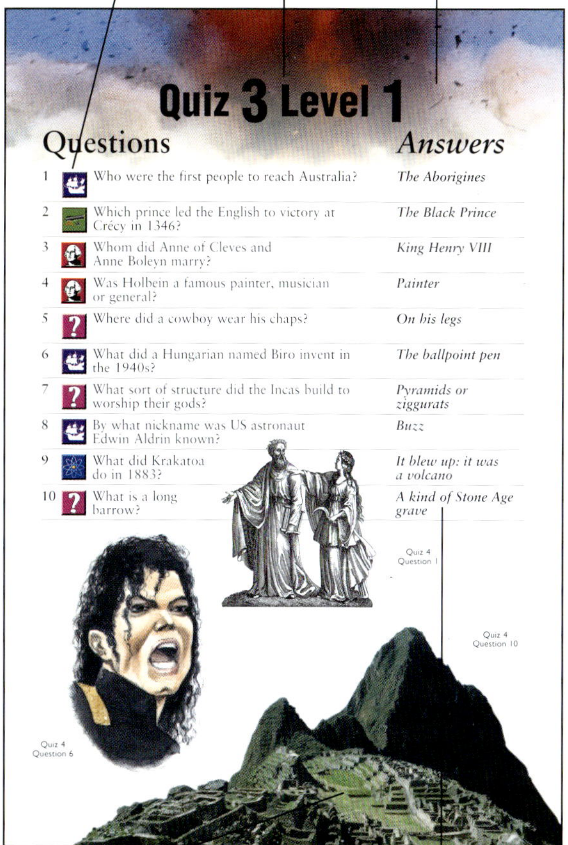

Picture clues 2
These visual clues will often help you get the answer – the label tells you which question they refer to

Answers
When doing the quizzes on your own, cover the answers with your hand or a piece of card

Quiz 1 Level 1

Questions		*Answers*
1	Was it Edison or Faraday who invented the light bulb?	*Edison*
2	What did Henry Ford make in his factories?	*Cars*
3	Were tea bags invented in the 1740s or the 1920s?	*The 1920s*
4	The Battle of Hastings is recorded on which famous tapestry?	*The Bayeux Tapestry*
5	In which sport was Babe Ruth a star?	*Baseball*
6	How did Sir Humphry Davy make coal mining safer?	*He invented a miner's safety lamp*
7	Which industry was revolutionized by the invention of the flying shuttle: weaving, transport, or mining?	*Weaving*
8	What did the ancient Egyptians use to sweeten food before the discovery of sugar?	*Honey*
9	What was Margot Fonteyn famous for: dancing, acting or singing?	*Dancing*
10	Which actor played James Bond in the first Bond film?	*Sean Connery*

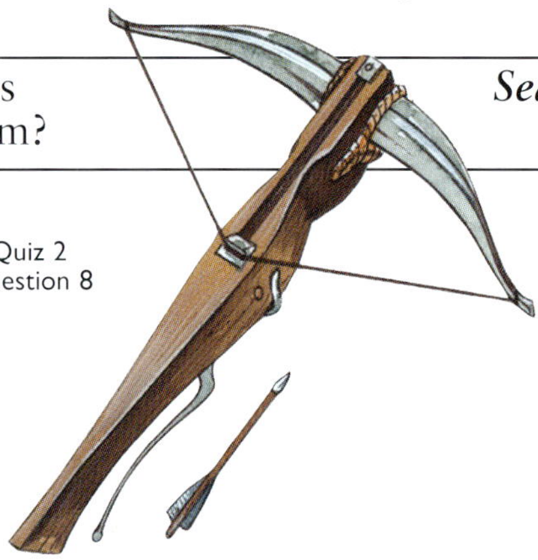

Quiz 2
Question 8

Quiz 2
Question 9

Quiz 2
Question 3

Quiz 2 Level 1

	Questions	Answers
1	Which people first brought the cat to Europe?	*The Romans*
2	In which war were the battles of Bull Run and Gettysburg?	*American Civil War*
3	Who was the first British monarch to travel in a train?	*Queen Victoria*
4	In which World War did poet Wilfred Owen fight?	*World War One*
5	Which Disney movie was based on a novel by French writer Victor Hugo?	*The Hunchback of Notre Dame*
6	Where does the expression 'checkmate' in chess come from?	*Arabic 'shah mat' 'the king is dead.'*
7	Roughly how many stone slabs are there in the Great Pyramid: 2,000, 20,000 or 2 million?	*2 million*
8	What is the arrow of a crossbow called?	*A bolt*
9	In which country did Ned Kelly become an outlaw?	*Australia*
10	What was special about the Heinkel He-178 plane, first flown in 1939?	*It was the first jet plane to fly*

Quiz 1 Question 6

Quiz 1, Question 4

Quiz 3 Level 1

Questions		Answers
1	Who were the first people to reach Australia?	*The Aborigines*
2	Which prince led the English to victory at Crécy in 1346?	*The Black Prince*
3	Whom did Anne of Cleves and Anne Boleyn marry?	*King Henry VIII*
4	Was Holbein a famous painter, musician or general?	*Painter*
5	Where did a cowboy wear his chaps?	*On his legs*
6	What did a Hungarian named Biro invent in the 1940s?	*The ballpoint pen*
7	What sort of structures did the Incas build to worship their gods?	*Pyramids or ziggurats*
8	By what nickname was US astronaut Edwin Aldrin known?	*Buzz*
9	What did Krakatoa do in 1883?	*It blew up: it was a volcano*
10	What is a long barrow?	*A kind of Stone Age grave*

Quiz 4
Question 1

Quiz 4
Question 6

Quiz 4
Question 10

Quiz 4 Level 1

Questions		Answers
1	What name was given to the Celtic priests?	*Druids*
2	What kind of letters made up the Viking alphabet?	*Runes*
3	What did a man named Dunlop invent in the 1880s?	*The air-filled tyre*
4	Who is the only English king called 'the Great'?	*Alfred the Great*
5	With what is the inventor Charles Babbage linked: computers, medicine or balloons?	*Computers*
6	Who recorded a best-selling album called *Thriller*?	*Michael Jackson*
7	Who were the first people to make paper?	*The Chinese*
8	Was dynamite an explosive or an early plastic?	*An explosive, invented in 1866*
9	Who returned to space in 1998 at the age of 77?	*John Glen*
10	Which empire was conquered by Pizarro?	*The Inca empire*

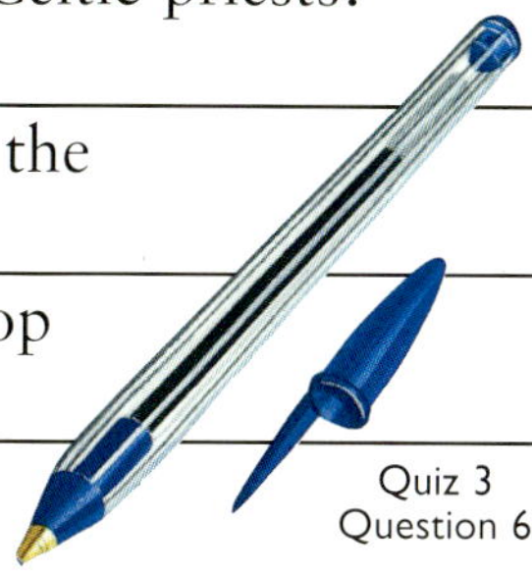

Quiz 3 Question 6

Quiz 3 Question 7

Quiz 5 Level 1

	Questions	Answers
1	Which musical instrument was invented by Adolphe Saxe?	*The saxophone*
2	Which explorer was first to reach the South Pole?	*Roald Amundsen*
3	What is an abacus used for?	*Mathematical calculations*
4	What was the name of the fleet sent by Spain against England in 1588?	*The Armada*
5	Which country used to be led by rulers called tsars?	*Russia*
6	In which foreign wars did King Richard I of England go to fight?	*The Crusades*
7	What do we call the ancient form of decoration using small pieces of tile or stone?	*Mosaic*
8	Where are the Crown Jewels?	*The Tower of London*
9	In which year were the very first Olympic games held: 776BC, AD776 or AD1000?	*776BC*
10	What event do the French people celebrate on July 14?	*The fall of the Bastille*

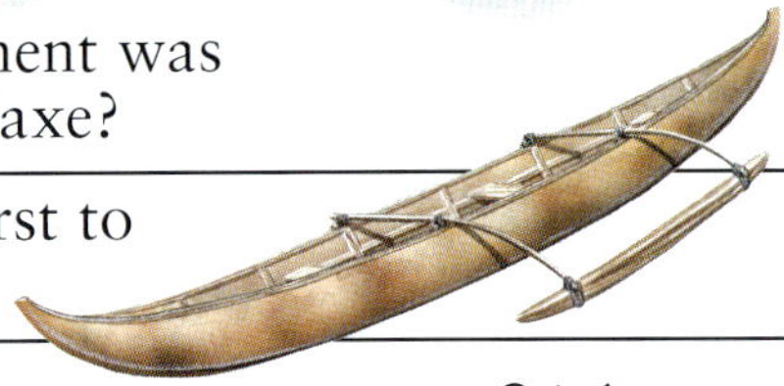

Quiz 6
Question 3

Quiz 6
Question 2

Quiz 6 Level 1

Questions		Answers
1	Which began first: the French Revolution or the American Revolution?	*The American (in 1775)*
2	How many wheels did a Celtic war chariot have?	*Two*
3	What kind of boats did Polynesians use for ocean voyages?	*Outrigger canoes*
4	Which Greek philosopher lived in a barrel?	*Diogenes*
5	Of which people was Genghis Khan a war leader?	*The Mongols*
6	In Shakespeare's play, who is the boy Juliet falls in love with?	*Romeo*
7	In which country did the ancient Olmecs live?	*Mexico*
8	Between which two countries does Offa's Dyke run?	*England and Wales*
9	Which Polish astronomer shocked people by saying that the Earth was not the centre of the Universe?	*Copernicus*
10	After which Greek victory in 490BC did a messenger run 42km to announce the good news?	*Marathon*

Quiz 5 Question 1

Quiz 5 Question 4

Quiz 5 Question 2

Quiz 7 Level 1

	Questions	Answers
1	With which queen did Julius Caesar and Mark Antony fall in love?	*Cleopatra*
2	It was once called Byzantium and then Constantinople. What do we call this city today?	*Istanbul*
3	What was Einstein's first name?	*Albert*
4	Was an autogyro an early helicopter-like plane or an early computer?	*An early helicopter-like plane*
5	Who was the ruler of the Greek gods?	*Zeus*
6	What kind of weapon was a tomahawk?	*An axe*
7	What was the name of the first jet airliner to fly?	*Comet*
8	Which came first: clay pots or metal tools?	*Clay pots*
9	Who wrote *Oliver Twist*?	*Charles Dickens*
10	Which material was accidentally made by ancient Egyptians when they lit a fire on a beach?	*Glass*

Quiz 8
Question 1

Quiz 8
Question 3

Quiz 8
Question 8

Quiz 8 Level 1

Questions / Answers

	Questions	Answers
1	What was DDT invented to do?	*Kill insect pests*
2	What were the Crusades?	*Religious wars against the Turks*
3	Where did Vasco da Gama sail in 1498?	*India*
4	Who commanded the British fleet at the Battle of Trafalgar in 1805?	*Nelson*
5	Which country built the *Nautilus*, the world's first nuclear submarine?	*The USA*
6	In which wars did the families of York and Lancaster fight each other?	*The Wars of the Roses*
7	Who was the first president of the United States?	*George Washington*
8	The people of which 'classical' empire worshipped the goddess Athene: Greece or Rome?	*Greece*
9	In the Bible, who built the Ark to save his family and the animals from the flood?	*Noah*
10	Which country developed the TGV high speed train?	*France*

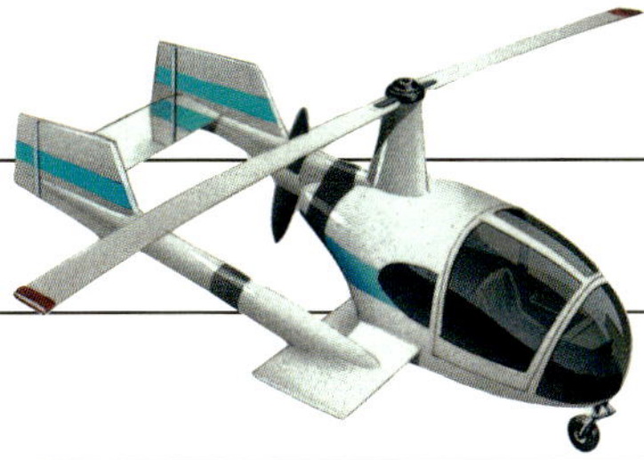

Quiz 7 Question 4

Quiz 7 Question 1

Quiz 7 Question 9

Quiz 9 Level 1

	Questions	Answers
1	Was a clipper a fast sailing ship, a surgical instrument, or a racehorse?	*A sailing ship*
2	Which branch of mathematics is named after the Arabic word *al-jabr*, to reduce?	*Algebra*
3	Who was the Greek slave who wrote the first animal fables in about 570BC?	*Aesop*
4	Who was the first man to orbit the Earth in a spacecraft?	*Yuri Gagarin (in 1961)*
5	When did people first use electric toasters: 1880s or 1920s?	*1920s*
6	What do the smiling and sad theatre masks stand for?	*Comedy and tragedy*
7	Which was the last to be used in Europe: knife, fork or spoon?	*Fork*
8	Was a minuet an old-fashioned dance, a gun, or an early clock?	*An old-fashioned dance*
9	Odin was the chief god of which race of people?	*Vikings, or Norsemen*
10	Of which city was Dick Whittington Lord Mayor?	*London*

Quiz 10
Question 5

Quiz 10
Question 7

Quiz 10 Level 1

	Questions	Answers
1	Which boxer said 'I am the Greatest'?	*Muhammad Ali*
2	Which two countries fought the Hundred Years' War?	*England and France*
3	According to legend, which Irish saint sailed to America in a leather boat in AD860?	*Brendan*
4	In which century was the French Revolution: 15th, 17th or 18th?	*18th century*
5	Which came first: electric street lights or gas lamps?	*Gas lamps*
6	What instruments did the Chinese use to pull out rotten teeth?	*Their fingers!*
7	Which sort of men used to joust on horses?	*Knights*
8	On which Mediterranean island was Napoleon Bonaparte born?	*Corsica*
9	Which Scottish inventor pioneered the television?	*John Logie Baird*
10	Which famous artist wrote in mirror writing (back to front)?	*Leonardo da Vinci*

Quiz 9
Question 9

Quiz 9
Question 10

Quiz 11 Level 1

	Questions	*Answers*
1	Which country developed the Space Shuttle?	*The USA*
2	Which empire was ruled by Darius the Great?	*The Persian Empire*
3	Who was the most famous escape artist of the 20th century?	*Harry Houdini*
4	What did Alexander Graham Bell invent in 1877?	*The telephone*
5	In which century did people first travel in cars?	*19th*
6	James Hargreaves invented the spinning jenny to do which job?	*Spin wool into yarn*
7	What did Volta invent in 1800?	*The electric battery*
8	Which English king was killed at the Battle of Bosworth in 1485?	*Richard III*
9	Which state in ancient Greece forced its people to live a strict life without any luxuries?	*Sparta*
10	In which sport did Jack Nicklaus find fame and fortune?	*Golf*

Quiz 12
Question 4

Quiz 12
Question 8

Quiz 12
Question 3

Quiz 12 Level 1

Questions		Answers
1	What was special about the British ship *Dreadnought* of 1906?	*It was the first modern battleship*
2	What was the painter Picasso's first name?	*Pablo*
3	Who was Queen of England at the time of the Spanish Armada?	*Queen Elizabeth I*
4	What kind of warplane is a B-52?	*A long-range bomber, used by the US Air Force*
5	Which fast food gets its name from a city in Germany?	*Hamburger (from Hamburg)*
6	Of which revolution was Robespierre a leader?	*The French Revolution*
7	Who was Robin Hood's sweetheart?	*Maid Marian*
8	What was a boneshaker?	*An early bicycle*
9	Who is the father of Britain's princes William and Harry?	*Charles, Prince of Wales*
10	For which country did Kenny Dalglish play international soccer?	*Scotland*

Quiz 11
Question 10

Quiz 11
Question 6

Quiz 11
Question 2

Quiz 13 Level 1

	Questions	Answers
1	What is a large ship powered by oars called?	*A galley*
2	Were hussars and dragoons foot-soldiers or horse-soldiers?	*Horse-soldiers*
3	Which spooky character was created by writer Bram Stoker?	*Dracula*
4	Which Greek conqueror founded the Egyptian city of Alexandria?	*Alexander the Great*
5	Which Asian invaders were led by Attila in 434?	*The Huns*
6	For what did the ancient Egyptians use a *shaduf*: moving stones or raising water?	*Raising water*
7	Which was the last of the single numbers to be invented?	*0 (zero)*
8	Was Elizabeth Fry a prison reformer or a cookery writer?	*A prison reformer*
9	What was a central market-place called in ancient Greece?	*The agora*
10	Why did cleaning carpets become simpler after 1876?	*The first carpet sweeper machine was invented*

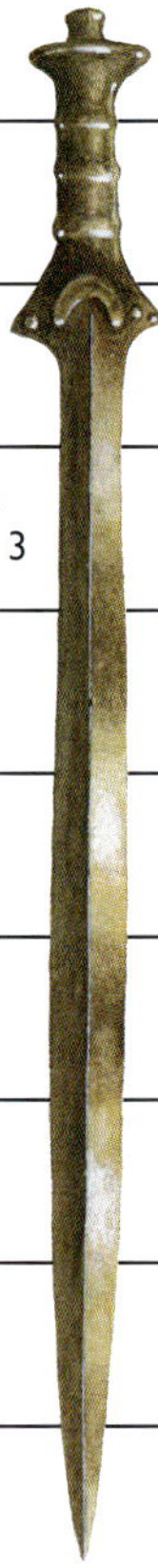

Quiz 14
Question 3

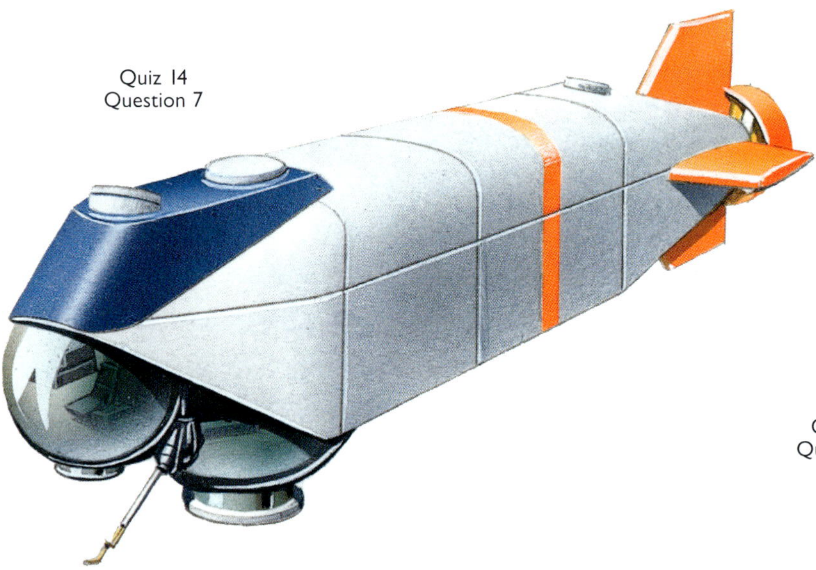

Quiz 14
Question 7

Quiz 14
Question 9

Quiz 14 Level 1

	Questions	*Answers*
1	What game did Denis Compton play?	*Cricket*
2	What surface was a fresco painted on?	*Fresh plaster*
3	Which came first, the Bronze Age or the Iron Age?	*The Bronze Age*
4	Where was the world's first dam built?	*Egypt*
5	What were stewponds used for in medieval monasteries?	*Raising fish for food*
6	Why were frogmen so called?	*Because they wore flippers to swim*
7	Where might you go in a bathyscaphe?	*Under the sea*
8	By what name was the outlaw William Bonney better known?	*Billy the Kid*
9	Infantrymen and cavalrymen are different types of what?	*Soldier*
10	Was Jesse James a real person?	*Yes*

Quiz 13
Question 1

Quiz 13
Question 5

Quiz 15 Level 1

	Questions	Answers
1	In which country was the composer Beethoven born?	*Germany*
2	From which country did the soldiers called hoplites come?	*Greece*
3	Who was the winged messenger of the Greek gods?	*Hermes*
4	What was President Lincoln's first name?	*Abraham*
5	What is roughly 4,600 million years old?	*The Earth*
6	Where was the Battle of Alamein fought in 1942?	*In the North African desert*
7	What name did Octavius take when he first became Roman Emperor?	*Augustus*
8	Ancient Egyptians wrote on a reed called papyrus. What modern word comes from this?	*Paper*
9	Of which country is Robert Burns the national poet?	*Scotland*
10	What was the Colosseum in Rome used for?	*Gladiator games*

Quiz 16
Question 5

Quiz 16
Question 8

Quiz 16 Level 1

Questions		Answers
1	What kind of car set the first world land speed record in 1898?	*An electric car*
2	Was Ted Hughes a poet, a cricketer, or a painter?	*A poet*
3	What kind of animal was Moby Dick?	*A white whale*
4	Which country was the first to use jet planes in war?	*Germany (during World War II)*
5	The Aborigines are the native people of which country?	*Australia*
6	Which race took place for the first time on the river Thames in 1829?	*Oxford and Cambridge Universities Boat Race*
7	Did Agatha Christie write funny stories, detective novels, or horror stories?	*Detective novels*
8	Which legendary English king was crowned when he pulled the sword *Excalibur* from the stone?	*King Arthur*
9	Which kind of mill was invented in Iran and came to Europe in about AD1000?	*The windmill*
10	Of what was John McAdam a pioneer?	*Roadbuilding*

Quiz 15 Question 4

Quiz 15 Question 10

Quiz 17 Level 1

Questions		Answers
1	What was the Archimedes screw used for?	*Raising water*
2	How many wings does a biplane have?	*Two*
3	Did Leonardo da Vinci ever build a flying machine?	*No: he drew plans for one, but it never flew*
4	In which country was the first cycle race held, in 1868?	*France*
5	Who was Douglas Bader?	*A British fighter pilot of World War II*
6	In which Anglo-Saxon poem does the monster Grendel appear?	*Beowulf*
7	Which sporting event was revived in 1896, and is held every four years?	*The Olympic Games*
8	What was a siege tower used for?	*Getting into a castle (over the walls)*
9	In which century were cannon first fired in battle – 11th, 14th or 16th?	*14th century*
10	Is it true that the first spectacles were held in the hand?	*Yes*

Quiz 18
Question 6

Quiz 18
Question 9

Quiz 18 Level 1

	Questions	Answers
1	Which planet was first seen in 1846?	*Neptune*
2	What was the name of Alexander the Great's favourite horse?	*Bucephalus*
3	Where was the empire ruled by Akbar the Great?	*India*
4	Which famous battle took place in 1916?	*Somme*
5	On which river was Rome built?	*The Tiber*
6	Who was in charge of the British forces at the Battle of Waterloo?	*The Duke of Wellington*
7	Don Bradman became Australia's most famous sportsman: in which sport?	*Cricket*
8	Which part of the body was used to measure an inch?	*The first thumb joint*
9	Who built the world's first practical aeroplane?	*The Wright Brothers*
10	In the Bible, which shepherd boy killed the giant Goliath?	*David*

Quiz 17
Question 2

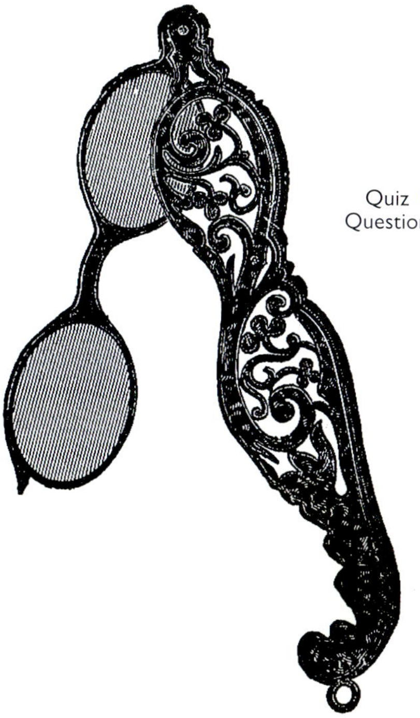

Quiz 17
Question 10

Quiz 17
Question 8

Quiz 19 Level 1

	Questions	Answers
1	What did William Wilberforce campaign to end in the British Empire?	*Slavery*
2	Ulysses is another name for which Greek hero?	*Odysseus*
3	What filled the first balloon to carry passengers?	*Hot air*
4	Which European country has the oldest parliament: Britain, Iceland or France?	*Iceland*
5	What was the job of the Roman god Mercury?	*Messenger of the gods*
6	What name is given to the ancient Egyptian form of picture writing?	*Hieroglyphs*
7	In which war were Haig and Pershing famous commanders?	*World War I*
8	Which country started the world's first public TV service in 1936?	*Britain*
9	Who was the first president of the United States?	*George Washington*
10	Which type of soldier fought in the Crusades?	*Knights*

Quiz 20
Question 9

Quiz 20 Level 1

Questions | *Answers*

	Questions	Answers
1	Which ocean did Charles Lindbergh fly across in 1927?	*The Atlantic*
2	How long is the great wall of China: 48km, 480km or 4800km?	*4800km*
3	Was Tarzan a real person?	*No*
4	What 'out of this world' event happened on 20 July 1969?	*Humans first landed on the moon*
5	Which Roman poet wrote the long poem called the *Aeneid*?	*Virgil*
6	What was the name of the ancient route which linked China with the west?	*The Silk Road*
7	What were troubadours in the Middle Ages?	*Wandering minstrels (musicians)*
8	Which Italian city has a famous leaning tower, completed in the 1360s?	*Pisa*
9	How long ago did the first farmers live?	*About 10,000 years ago*
10	In which year did the Romans successfully invade Britain?	*AD43*

Quiz 19
Question 5

Quiz 19
Question 10

Quiz 21 Level

Questions		Answers
1	Do sharks have bones?	*No, their skeletons are made of gristly cartilage*
2	Was Beethoven a Dutch painter or a German composer?	*A German composer*
3	What organization was founded by Robert Baden-Powell?	*The Boy Scouts*
4	When did medieval soldiers use scaling ladders?	*When attacking a castle (to climb up the walls)*
5	In what year was Mount Everest first climbed?	*1953*
6	Which Greek writer wrote the *Iliad*?	*Homer*
7	What is the famous Shakespearean theatre in London called?	*The Globe*
8	For what was Wilhelm Röntgen famous?	*He discovered X-rays*
9	Which country was called Cathay by Europeans?	*China*
10	Was a trebuchet a giant catapult, a warhorse, or a kind of ship?	*A giant catapult used for hurling stones*

Quiz 22 Question 8

Quiz 22 Question 1

Quiz 22 Level 1

	Questions	Answers
1	Which castle in London was built at around the time of William the Conqueror?	*The Tower of London*
2	Who is the patron saint of Ireland?	*St. Patrick*
3	Who discovered Botany Bay?	*Captain Cook*
4	Which king was killed at the Battle of Hastings?	*King Harold*
5	What kind of weapon was a ballista?	*An ancient missile launcher*
6	Which English writer wrote *The Canterbury Tales*, about pilgrims on their way to Canterbury?	*Chaucer*
7	Which white marble mausoleum at Agra, India, took 20,000 men over 20 years to complete?	*Taj Mahal*
8	About when did the Iron Age begin: 19,000BC, 1900BC or 190BC?	*1900BC*
9	What was the Kon-Tiki which crossed the Pacific: a raft, a balloon, or a canoe?	*A raft*
10	Which European people sailed in longships?	*The Vikings*

Quiz 21 Question 6

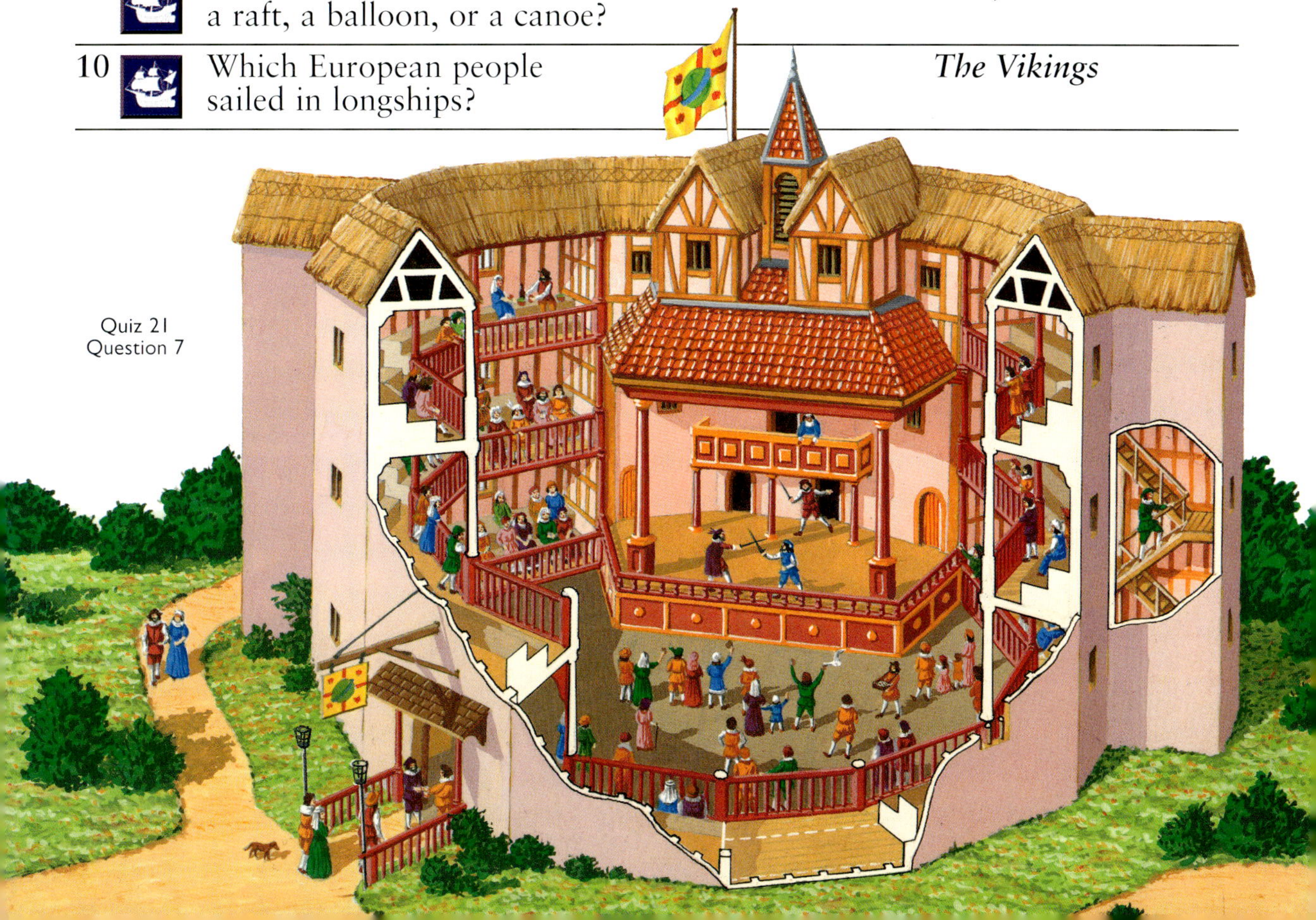

Quiz 21 Question 7

Quiz 23 Level 1

	Questions	Answers
1	Who painted the *Mona Lisa*?	*Leonardo da Vinci*
2	Was the Mustang a famous fighter plane or a kind of gun?	*A US fighter plane, used in World War II*
3	Who travelled non-stop around the world in a balloon in 1999?	*Brian James and Bertrand Picard*
4	Who created the Church of England to divorce his first wife?	*King Henry VIII*
5	Who in the Bible lost his strength when his hair was cut?	*Samson*
6	Which famous explorer was killed in Hawaii in 1779?	*Captain Cook*
7	What was the first antibiotic drug?	*Penicillin*
8	In which country is a warrior called El Cid a national hero?	*Spain*
9	Which of the Seven Wonders of the Ancient World was in the city of Babylon?	*The Hanging Gardens*
10	Who wrote *Pride and Prejudice*?	*Jane Austen*

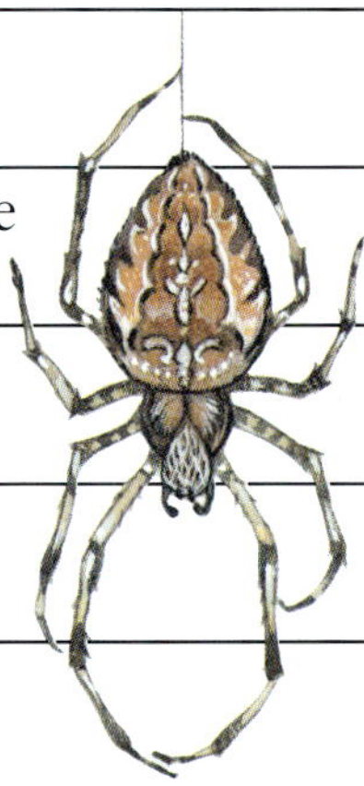

Quiz 24
Question 4

Quiz 24
Question 2

Quiz 24
Question 8

Quiz 24 Level 1

	Questions	Answers
1	At which battle did the Indians defeat General Custer?	*Battle of the Little Big Horn*
2	Giuseppe Garibaldi is a famous soldier in which European country?	*Italy*
3	To where did a Viking named Leif Ericsson sail?	*North America*
4	Which animal inspired King Robert the Bruce of Scotland to try again?	*A spider*
5	Which tramp with a bowler hat and cane was much loved by silent movie-goers?	*Charlie Chaplin*
6	What animal gave milk to the twins Romulus and Remus when they were left to die?	*A she-wolf*
7	Which naturalist sailed around the world in *The Beagle*?	*Charles Darwin*
8	For what occupation was Jesus trained?	*Carpentry*
9	In which war was the Battle of the Somme?	*World War I (1914-1918)*
10	Did Sir Francis Chichester sail around the world or fly the Pacific in a balloon?	*He sailed around the world, in 1967*

Quiz 23
Question 6

Quiz 23
Question 4

Quiz 25 Level 1

Questions		Answers
1	Which major world religion was founded by the Indian Prince Gautama?	*Buddhism*
2	Who is supposed to have said 'A horse! A horse! My kingdom for a horse!'?	*Richard III*
3	Who sailed in the *Endeavour*?	*Captain Cook*
4	Who led his army from Greece to the Himalayas?	*Alexander the Great*
5	Who discovered the antibiotic penicillin?	*Alexander Fleming*
6	What were the penny black and the penny red?	*British postage stamps*
7	Which Roman emperor was killed by Brutus?	*Julius Caesar*
8	What was the first name of the famous female scientist, Curie?	*Marie*
9	What cleaning device was invented by James M. Spangler in 1908?	*Vacuum cleaner*
10	What animal did Arab cavalrymen ride before horses?	*Camels*

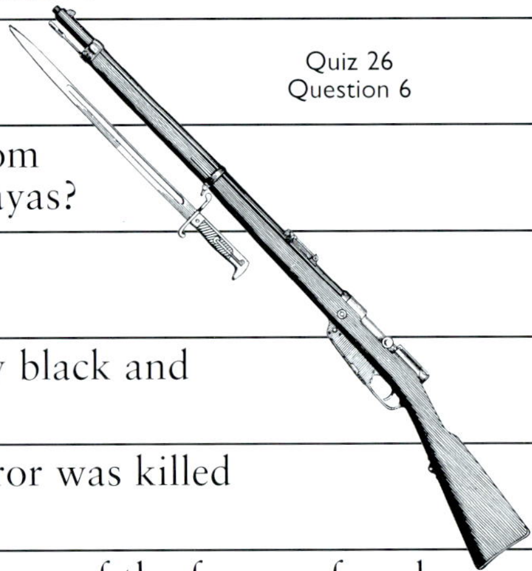

Quiz 26
Question 6

Quiz 26
Question 9

Quiz 26
Question 5

Quiz 26 Level 1

	Questions	Answers
1	Which volcano covered the Italian town of Pompeii with ash in AD62?	*Vesuvius*
2	Which coast did Matthew Flinders explore in about 1800?	*Australian*
3	Which French king built the Palace of Versailles?	*Louis XIV (the Fourteenth)*
4	Which Irish saint was once captured and sold as a slave?	*Patrick*
5	Who led the Communist Revolution in China?	*Mao Tse-tung (Mao Zedong)*
6	Where did a soldier fix a bayonet?	*On the end of his rifle*
7	Which continent is named after Amerigo Vespucci (1454-1512)?	*America*
8	Which country used to have an emperor called the kaiser?	*Germany*
9	What were 'clipper' ships famous for carrying?	*Tea*
10	Which god in Hindu mythology has an elephant's head?	*Ganesh*

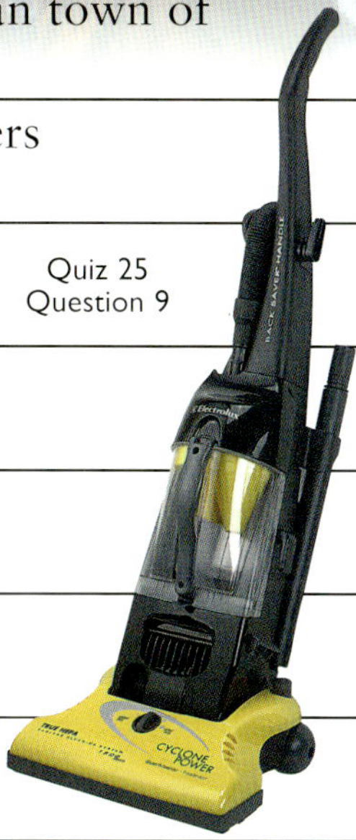

Quiz 25
Question 9

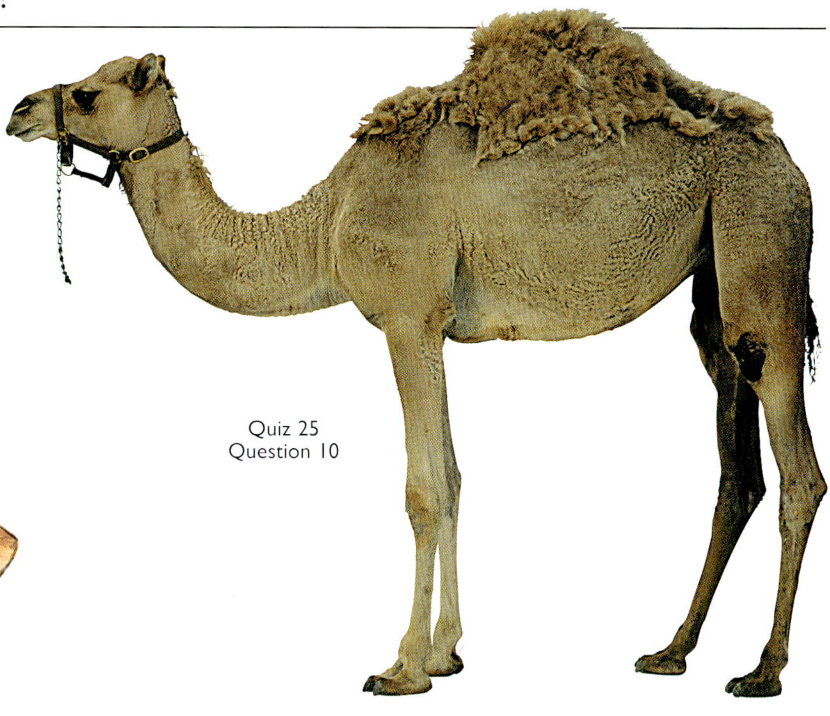
Quiz 25
Question 10

Quiz 25
Question 7

Quiz 27 Level 1

	Questions	Answers
1	Who wrote *Treasure Island?*	*Robert Louis Stevenson*
2	Was Dr Crippen a famous murderer or the inventor of Snakes and Ladders?	*A famous murderer*
3	Who was nicknamed the 'Lady of the Lamp' during the Crimean war?	*Florence Nightingale*
4	How many of Magellan's ships sailed home after circling the world in 1522?	*One*
5	What was the first mass-produced car in 1908?	*The Ford Model-T*
6	What changed the way books were made in the 1400s?	*The invention of printing with movable type*
7	How many children has Queen Elizabeth II of Britain?	*Four*
8	Which country had the first roadside petrol pump?	*The USA (in 1906)*
9	Which Russian composer wrote the 1812 Overture?	*Tchaikovsky*
10	To which country did Marco Polo journey?	*China*

Quiz 28
Question 3

Quiz 28
Question 8

Quiz 28 Level 1

	Questions	Answers
1	Did the first bicycles have pedals?	*No, they were were pushed along*
2	In which country were Europe's first banks?	*Italy*
3	What was the system called under which serfs worked for the lord?	*The feudal system*
4	Who tried to blow up the British Houses of Parliament in 1605?	*Guy Fawkes*
5	What kind of craft was a Zeppelin?	*An airship*
6	Who invented the lightning rod?	*Benjamin Franklin*
7	Which English county is named after the East Saxons?	*Essex*
8	Hoplite soldiers from which country fought in a phalanx?	*Greece*
9	How long was the pike used by Alexander the Great's soldiers: 1 metre, 3 metres or 6 metres?	*6 metres*
10	Was Leonardo da Vinci born near Florence, Italy, or in Vienna, Austria?	*Near Florence, Italy*

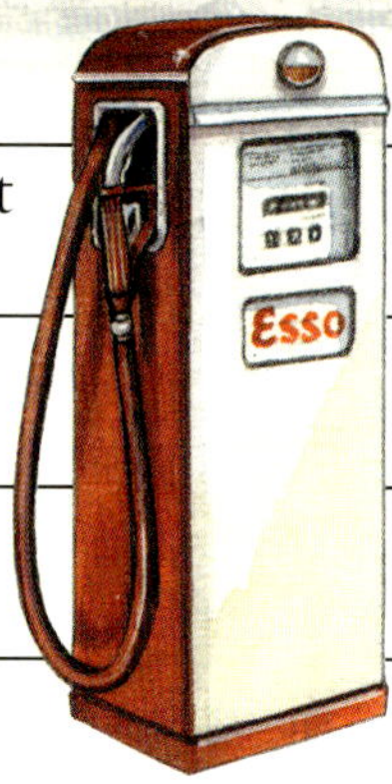

Quiz 27
Question 8

Quiz 27
Question 3

Quiz 27
Question 5

Quiz 29 Level 1

Questions		Answers
1	Which people invented the magnetic compass?	*The Chinese*
2	Which holy book was first written down by the prophet Muhammad?	*The Koran*
3	Which country attacked Pearl Harbor in 1941?	*Japan*
4	Which explorer, who discovered America, sailed in the *Santa Maria*?	*Christopher Columbus*
5	In which Greek city is the Parthenon?	*Athens*
6	What fell on Newton's head, according to one story?	*An apple (making him think about gravity)*
7	In which war were V-1 flying bombs used?	*World War II (1939-1945)*
8	Which great river flowed through ancient Egypt?	*The Nile*
9	What device helped the Greeks to capture the city of Troy?	*A wooden horse*
10	In which century did the Industrial Revolution begin?	*18th (1700s)*

Quiz 30 Question 10

Quiz 30 Question 2

Quiz 30 Question 8

Quiz 30 Level 1

	Questions	Answers
1	Which two countries began a 'space race' in 1957?	*USSR and USA*
2	Who laid down his cloak to keep Queen Elizabeth I's feet dry?	*Sir Walter Raleigh*
3	When were X-rays discovered?	*1895*
4	Which Johnson was a famous aviator: Amy, Jack or Lyndon?	*Amy Johnson*
5	Who was the Norse god of thunder?	*Thor*
6	Which Roman emperor ordered the building of a frontier wall across northern England in AD122?	*Hadrian*
7	Which great French scientist made the first vaccine against rabies?	*Louis Pasteur*
8	What is a blunderbuss?	*A old type of gun*
9	During the Ice Age sea levels dropped. How did this help the first people to reach America?	*They crossed from Asia on exposed land*
10	In which country is the kimono a form of national dress?	*Japan*

Quiz 29
Question 4

Quiz 29
Question 9

Quiz 31 Level 1

Questions		Answers
1	Which mountain range did Hannibal famously cross with his army and their elephants?	*The Alps*
2	Which sea captain sailed in the *Golden Hind*?	*Francis Drake*
3	Is the Humboldt current a part of a TV set or water in the ocean?	*It's a cold ocean current off South America*
4	Who founded the American state of Pennsylvania?	*William Penn*
5	What was a 'powder monkey' on an old sailing warship?	*A boy who carried gunpowder*
6	About when did the first modern humans appear: 1,500,000BC, 150,000BC or 15,000BC?	*150,000BC*
7	What kind of farm machine did Cyrus McCormick invent?	*A mechanical harvester*
8	Was the Egyptian pharaoh Tutankhamun buried in a pyramid?	*No – he was buried in a tomb*
9	In the book *Gulliver's Travels*, are the people from Lilliput large or small?	*Small*
10	Who wore bellbottom trousers: sailors, soldiers, or airmen?	*Sailors*

Quiz 32 Question 8

Quiz 32 Question 2

Quiz 32 Level 1

Questions		Answers
1	Why did early steamships have sails as well as engines?	*In case the engines broke down or ran out of fuel*
2	Of what were the roofs of Bronze Age houses made?	*Thatch (straw)*
3	Which female East Anglian leader rebelled against Roman rule in AD122?	*Boudicca*
4	In which year was the first all-iron bridge built at Coalbrookdale, England?	*1779*
5	Who won the battle of Saratoga in 1777?	*The Americans, when the British surrendered*
6	Who wrote the great Greek tragic play *Oedipus Rex*?	*Sophocles*
7	Who commanded *HMS Bounty* on a voyage to the Pacific in 1787?	*Captain William Bligh*
8	Who composed *The Planets* suite between 1914 and 1917 ?	*Gustav Holst*
9	Who did Queen Elizabeth I of England marry?	*No-one*
10	What was the last planet in the solar system to be discovered?	*Pluto, in 1930*

Quiz 31
Question 6

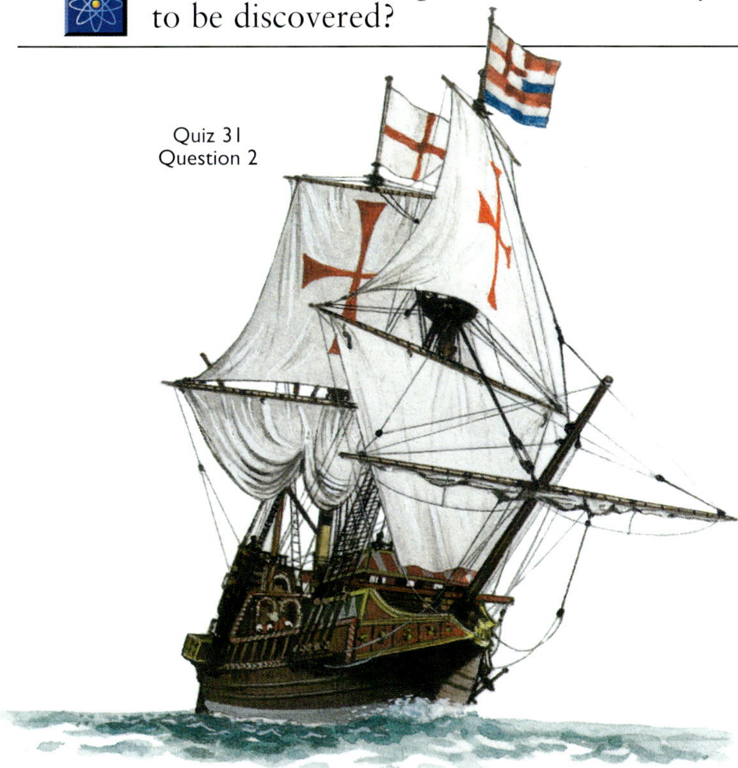

Quiz 31
Question 2

Quiz 31
Question 2

Quiz 33 Level 1

Questions		*Answers*
1	Why did explorers often carry chickens and goats on board ships?	*For eggs and goats' milk*
2	What is a religious man who lives in a monastery called?	*A monk*
3	Was Amelia Earhart a famous flier, a lone sailor, or a mountaineer?	*A famous flier*
4	What do Henry Irving, Laurence Olivier and John Gielgud have in common?	*Acting (all three became famous actors)*
5	In the Bible, which unwilling prophet was swallowed by a whale?	*Jonah*
6	Who was a famous English writer in the 1600s: John Milton, John Le Carré or John Keats?	*John Milton*
7	Which continent did Columbus hope to find by sailing west?	*Asia*
8	Who wrote *The Faerie Queene* in the 1500s?	*Edmund Spenser*
9	For what was Nijinsky famous?	*Ballet dancing*
10	Who discovered the principle of buoyancy in about 250BC?	*Archimedes*

Quiz 34
Question 1

Quiz 34
Question 9

Quiz 34 Level 1

	Questions	*Answers*
1	The people of which ancient 'classical' civilization wore togas?	***Rome***
2	Which composer went deaf in his later years?	***Beethoven***
3	When did the ancient Egyptians devise the 365-day calendar?	***2500BC***
4	Did Columbus make just one voyage to the Americas?	***No, he made four***
5	Which country did Napoleon invade in 1812?	***Russia***
6	When did Euclid write *Elements of Geometry*, one of the most influential mathematics books ever?	***300BC***
7	What was the nickname of the American Confederate general Thomas Jackson?	***Stonewall***
8	When was gunpowder first used in battle in Europe: 1346, 1446 or 1546?	***1346***
9	Which Scottish king killed King Duncan, but was himself killed by Duncan's son, Malcolm III?	***Macbeth***
10	Which king ordered the Domesday Book to be made in England?	***William I***

Quiz 33
Question 2

Quiz 33
Question 3

Quiz 35 Level 1

Questions / *Answers*

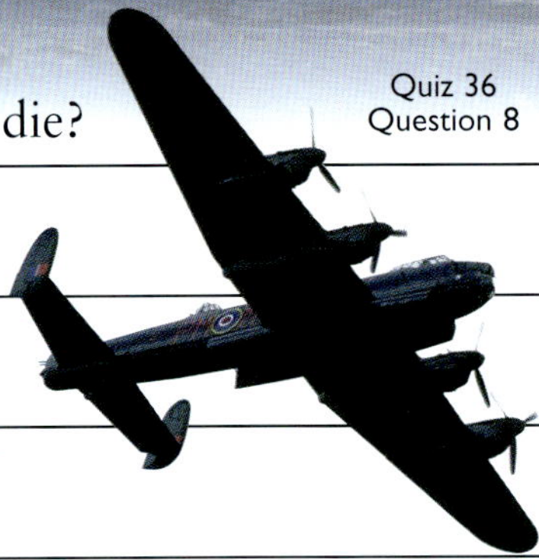
Quiz 36 Question 8

	Questions	Answers
1	Who were the only two people in the Bible not to die?	*Elijah and Enoch*
2	When was the first microscope invented?	*1590*
3	Who painted the roof of the Sistine Chapel?	*Michelangelo*
4	In what year was the first pistol made?	*1540*
5	The mythical monster the minotaur is a man with the head of what: a lion, a bull or an eagle?	*A bull*
6	What was the piece of armour that protected a knight's legs called?	*Greaves*
7	What were World War I trenches?	*Defensive ditches*
8	In which Italian town was Shakespeare's play *Romeo and Juliet* set?	*Verona*
9	What was a caravel?	*A kind of sailing ship*
10	What was the name of the winged horse in Greek legend?	*Pegasus*

Quiz 36 Question 4

Quiz 36 Question 7

Quiz 36 Level 1

		Questions	Answers
1		At the tip of which continent is Cape Horn?	*South America*
2		What was a Sopwith Camel in World War I?	*A fighter plane*
3		Who was the first Englishman to sail around the world?	*Sir Walter Raleigh*
4		What was a penny farthing?	*An early bicycle*
5		Was a Tin Lizzie an early car or an early washing machine?	*An early car*
6		In what year was the first steam boat sailed by Claude d'Abbans in France: 1683, 1783 or 1883?	*1783*
7		What was a Roman soldier in charge of 80 men called?	*A centurion*
8		What were Lancasters and Flying Fortresses?	*Bombers used in World War II (1939-1945)*
9		Which ocean did explorers cross to reach India from East Africa?	*The Indian Ocean*
10		Who was the king of the Roman gods?	*Jupiter*

Quiz 35
Question 7

Quiz 37 Level 1

#	Questions	Answers
1	Which queen of England ruled from 1837 to 1901?	*Queen Victoria*
2	What made sailors suffer from the disease called scurvy?	*Not eating fresh fruit and vegetables*
3	Which country celebrates its independence on the 4th of July?	*The United States*
4	Of which country was Helmut Kohl leader until 1998?	*Germany*
5	What was the first living creature sent into space in 1957: a dog, a monkey or a rabbit?	*A Russian dog named Laika*
6	What is the traditional date for Guy Fawkes fireworks and bonfires in Britain?	*November 5*
7	Was Columbus born in Spain or Italy?	*Italy*
8	Was a pike a long spearlike weapon or a helmet with a spike on top?	*A long spearlike weapon*
9	In 1642 Abel Tasman landed on a new island that he called Van Diemen's Land. What is it called now?	*Tasmania*
10	Which Indian leader was known as the Mahatma or 'Great Soul'?	*Gandhi*

Quiz 38
Question 5

Quiz 38
Question 4

Quiz 38 Level 1

	Questions	Answers
1	How many actors speak a monologue?	*One*
2	Which German general of World War II was nicknamed The Desert Fox?	*Rommel*
3	This country was once called Siam: what is its modern name?	*Thailand*
4	Explorers in South America caught and ate cavies: what were cavies?	*Guinea pigs*
5	Where did ammonites live: in trees, on the ground or under the sea?	*Under the sea*
6	What were U-boats?	*German submarines*
7	Who was the first pope?	*The apostle St Peter*
8	Which country used Zero fighters during World War II?	*Japan*
9	Who is the odd one out of these three leaders: Truman, Macmillan, Bush?	*Macmillan (British PM not US president)*
10	Against whom did Richard the Lionheart fight in the Crusades?	*Saladin*

Quiz 37
Question 7

Quiz 37
Question 8

Quiz 39 Level 2

Questions			Answers
1		Who made the first successful wireless in 1895?	*Guglielmo Marconi*
2		Who wrote *The Wind in the Willows*?	*Kenneth Grahame*
3		What kind of instrument is a clavichord?	*A keyboard instrument*
4		Who led the Jewish people from captivity in Egypt to Palestine?	*Moses*
5		What is the traditional dress worn by the Japanese?	*The kimono*
6		Who brought the first horses to North America?	*The Spanish*
7		Why were canaries once taken down coal mines?	*To give warning of dangerous gases*
8		What kind of plane was a Stuka?	*A dive-bomber*
9		What kind of armour was made out of tiny metal rings?	*Chain mail*
10		What pack animal was known as 'the ship of the desert'?	*The camel*
11		What is the companion story to Lewis Carroll's *Alice in Wonderland*?	Through the Looking-Glass
12		What was St Paul's name before he converted to Christianity?	*Saul*
13		James Cook's first ship was a collier. What kind of ship was this?	*One made for carrying coal*
14		In which sport was Rod Laver famous?	*Tennis*
15		In 1769 a French priest designed a waistcoat filled with cork. What was it?	*The first lifebelt*

Quiz 40
Question 1

Quiz 40
Question 10

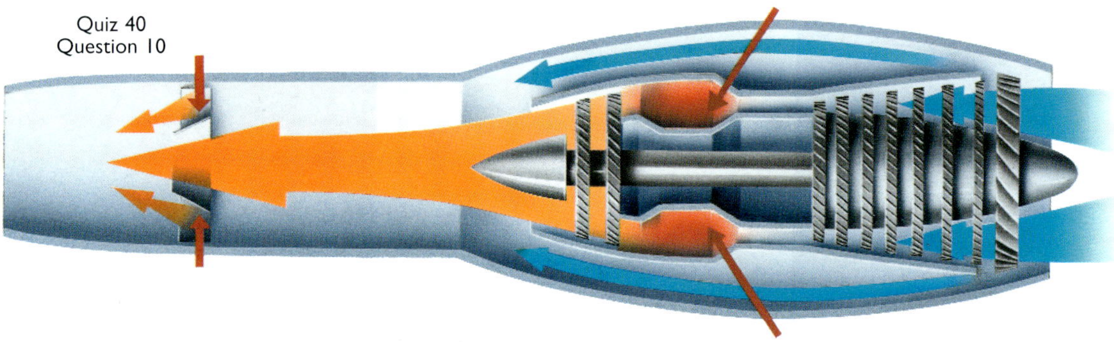

Quiz 40 Level 2

Questions		Answers
1	Was Charlie Chaplin American or British?	*British*
2	What name was given to the poisonous juice which Jean Nicot extracted from tobacco in 1562?	*Nicotine*
3	What was a castle's portcullis?	*A barrier lowered to block a gateway*
4	Who set out his idea of an ideal state in his book *Utopia*?	*Thomas More*
5	Was the 19th-century novelist George Eliot a man or a woman?	*A woman (Mary Ann Evans)*
6	In which city is the Kremlin?	*Moscow*
7	When did work begin on the first Channel Tunnel: 1751, 1882 or 1974?	*1882*
8	What kind of weapon is a bayonet?	*A blade fitted to the end of a rifle*
9	When did sailors first use the magnetic compass: 1000 BC, AD1000 or 1500?	*AD1000*
10	What new kind of aircraft engine was developed by Frank Whittle in the 1930s?	*The jet engine*
11	How many British kings have been called Charles?	*Two*
12	Who wrote a *History of the World* while in prison in 1614?	*Walter Raleigh*
13	What part of a knight's armour was the basinet?	*Helmet*
14	Who wrote the novel *Far From the Madding Crowd*?	*Thomas Hardy*
15	Who tried to invade Russia in 1812?	*Napoleon*

Quiz 39 Question 5

Quiz 39 Question 10

Quiz 39 Question 9

Quiz 41 Level 2

Questions		*Answers*
1	What is the name of the boy thieves' ringleader in *Oliver Twist*?	*Fagin*
2	What were the initials of Lawrence of Arabia?	*T.E.*
3	What kind of weapon was a ballista?	*A giant crossbow*
4	Who invented the phonograph, an early kind of record player?	*Thomas Edison*
5	Of which Native American people was Sitting Bull a leader?	*Hunkpapa Teton Sioux*
6	Which planet in our Solar System was discovered in 1930?	*Pluto*
7	What are teachers called in the Jewish religion?	*Rabbis*
8	Which famous structure was built by an Indian emperor as a tomb for his wife?	*The Taj Mahal*
9	Which two teams played in the first cricket Test Match?	*England and Australia*
10	Which World War II fighter pilot had false legs?	*Douglas Bader*
11	Which US state was founded by William Penn?	*Pennsylvania*
12	Which film actress did baseball star Joe di Maggio marry?	*Marilyn Monroe*
13	What do architects use a buttress for ?	*To support a wall*
14	Which Brazilian football player was born Edson Arantes do Nascimento?	*Pelé*
15	When did plastic surgery begin: 2,000 years ago, 1,000 years ago or 10 years ago?	*2,000 years ago*

Quiz 42
Question 4

Quiz 42
Question 2

Quiz 42
Question 3

Quiz 42 Level 2

Questions		Answers
1	Who painted the famous picture *Water-Lilies* in about 1921?	*Claude Monet*
2	Which Scotsman made the first steam engine to use cranks and pistons in 1769?	*James Watt*
3	Which Soviet leader called himself 'Man of Steel'?	*Josef Stalin*
4	What is the symbol of Canada?	*A maple leaf*
5	Who designed a helicopter, a parachute and an armoured car over 500 years ago?	*Leonardo da Vinci*
6	Which Australian folk hero was hanged in Melbourne in 1880?	*Ned Kelly*
7	In which city is the Empire State Building?	*New York*
8	Which war was ended by the Treaty of Appomattox?	*American Civil War*
9	What birds live at the Tower of London?	*Ravens*
10	Who became British prime minister in 1940?	*Winston Churchill*
11	Who was Elizabeth I's mother?	*Anne Boleyn*
12	Who first put forward the theory that creatures evolved through natural selection?	*Charles Darwin*
13	From which country did Ming Dynasty porcelain come?	*China*
14	What was the nickname of World War I German pilot Baron von Richthofen?	*The Red Baron*
15	Which South Seas volcano blew up in 1883?	*Krakatoa*

Quiz 41 Question 12

Quiz 41 Question 4

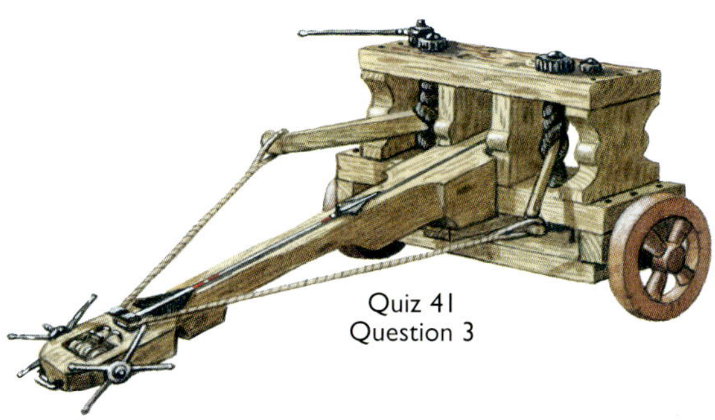
Quiz 41 Question 3

Quiz 43 Level 2

Questions — *Answers*

	Questions	Answers
1	Who was known as 'the Lady with the Lamp'?	*Florence Nightingale*
2	Which Old English poem features a man-eating monster called Grendel?	Beowulf
3	What was the job of a medieval armourer?	*To mend and make weapons and armour*
4	Who built the Menai Straits Bridge in Wales?	*Thomas Telford*
5	In which city is Michelangelo's statue of David?	*Florence*
6	Which country did Confucius come from?	*China*
7	How many symphonies did Beethoven write?	*Nine*
8	In which city is St Paul's Cathedral?	*London*
9	What was a Chinese junk?	*A sailing ship*
10	Who built the first electric dynamo, or generator, in 1831?	*Michael Faraday*
11	In which country did samurai warriors live?	*Japan*
12	What was celebrated on VE Day in 1945?	*Victory in Europe*
13	In which country was newspaper tycoon Rupert Murdoch born?	*Australia*
14	Which canal almost became the centre of a war in 1956?	*The Suez Canal*
15	What was the ditch around a castle called?	*A moat*

Quiz 44
Question 15

Quiz 44
Question 10

Quiz 44
Question 8

Quiz 44 Level 2

Questions		Answers
1	In which year was the silicon chip invented: 1925, 1955 or 1975?	*1975*
2	Which kind of musical work was Giuseppe Verdi most famous for?	*Opera*
3	Which US president was forced to resign in 1974?	*Richard Nixon*
4	What was the nickname of pirate Edward Teach?	*Blackbeard*
5	Who wrote the novel *Jane Eyre*?	*Charlotte Brontë*
6	Why was Marco Polo nicknamed 'Marco Millions'?	*Because he told a million tales*
7	Who took part in the Six-Day War of 1967?	*Israelis and Arabs*
8	What kind of engine was Thomas Newcomen famous for inventing?	*Steam engine*
9	Which Wonder of the World was built on the orders of Egyptian king Cheops?	*The Great Pyramid*
10	How many sets of wings had a triplane?	*Three*
11	Of which country was Charles de Gaulle the president?	*France*
12	How many voyages did Christopher Columbus make to America?	*Four*
13	Who was the first man to fly in space?	*Yuri Gagarin*
14	Who was emperor of China when Marco Polo arrived in 1275?	*Kublai Khan*
15	Which Communist leader ruled China from 1949?	*Mao Tse-tung*

Quiz 43
Question 4

Quiz 43
Question 10

Quiz 45 Level 2

	Questions	Answers
1	What did Indian leader M.K. Gandhi's title 'Mahatma' mean?	*'Great Soul'*
2	What name was given to the electro-magnetic rays which can see inside the human body?	*X-rays*
3	Which country is the setting for Shakespeare's play *Macbeth*?	*Scotland*
4	In which country were rockets probably invented over 700 years ago?	*China*
5	Who was the first woman to swim the English Channel?	*Gertrude Ederle*
6	Which country was reformed by Kemal Atatürk during the 1920s?	*Turkey*
7	What short-cut did Magellan take from the Atlantic to the Pacific?	*The straits now named after him*
8	In what way was the longbow a better weapon than the crossbow?	*It could be loaded much more quickly*
9	Is a clarinet a brass or woodwind instrument?	*Woodwind*
10	Of which country did Fidel Castro become leader in 1959?	*Cuba*
11	What was the job of a knight's squire?	*He was the knight's servant*
12	Who was the youngest ever president of the USA?	*John F. Kennedy*
13	Who is the patron saint of Scotland?	*St Andrew*
14	In which African desert is the ancient city of Timbuktu?	*The Sahara*
15	What pushed steamships along before the invention of the screw propeller?	*Paddle wheels*

Quiz 46
Question 2

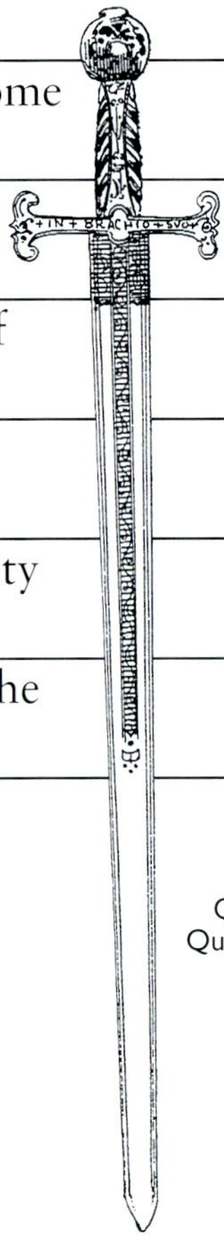

Quiz 46
Question 14

Quiz 46 Level 2

Questions		Answers
1	Which Muslim leader was the founder of Pakistan?	*Mohammed Ali Jinnah*
2	In which forest did the outlaw Robin Hood take refuge?	*Sherwood*
3	What country did European explorers call Cathay?	*China*
4	Who first split light into the colours of the rainbow using a prism?	*Isaac Newton*
5	Which US president are teddy bears named after?	*Theodore (Teddy) Roosevelt*
6	Who was the first black heavyweight boxing champion of the world?	*Jack Johnson*
7	Which bloodsucking fiend was created by novelist Bram Stoker in 1897?	*Dracula*
8	Which two countries made the agreement called the *entente cordiale* in 1904?	*Britain and France*
9	What do we call a picture painted on a wall?	*A mural*
10	In which year did someone first land on the Moon?	*1969*
11	Which modern invention first appeared in 1920: television, tea bags or telephones?	*Tea bags*
12	Who invented the system of measuring temperature in which water boils at 100 degrees?	*Anders Celsius*
13	Which native people of Nepal worked as porters and guides for European climbers in the Himalayas?	*Sherpas*
14	What is the pommel of a sword?	*The knob at the top of the hilt*
15	In which country did the Boxer Rebellion take place in 1900?	*China*

Quiz 45 Question 15

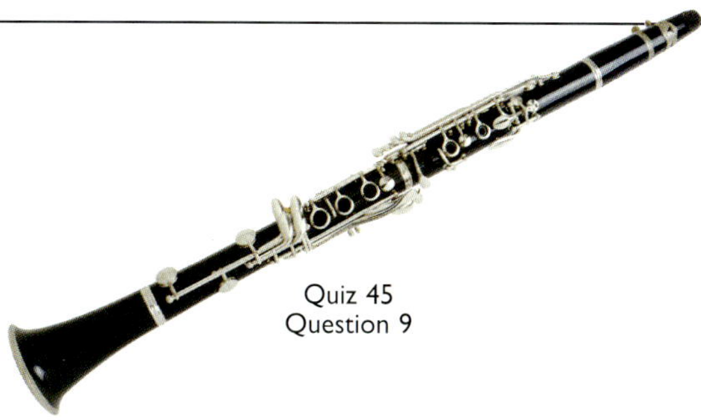

Quiz 45 Question 9

Quiz 47 Level 2

	Questions	*Answers*
1	Who wrote the poem beginning 'I wandered lonely as a cloud'?	*William Wordsworth*
2	Which people founded the city of Tenochtitlán in about 1325?	*Aztec*
3	What kind of air transport did the Montgolfier brothers invent in the 1780s?	*The hot-air balloon*
4	Which South American country was named after the freedom fighter Simón Bolívar?	*Bolivia*
5	What is the name of the cape at the southern tip of South America?	*Cape Horn*
6	What use was found for coal gas in the 1940s?	*Street lighting*
7	When were black slaves first taken to the Caribbean: 1501, 1601 or 1701?	*1501*
8	What is a mercenary soldier?	*One who fights for anyone who pays him*
9	What nickname was given to Ivan IV of Russia?	*The Terrible*
10	Why were English coins given milled edges in 1562?	*To stop people clipping bits off them*
11	What part of the world was explored by a bathyscaphe in 1960?	*The Pacific Ocean floor*
12	Which instrument was invented by Adolphe Sax in 1846?	*The saxophone*
13	Who was president of the USA for most of the World War II?	*Franklin D. Roosevelt*
14	Was Botticelli a sculptor, a painter or a musician?	*A painter*
15	Which American dancer is famous for 'singin' in the rain'?	*Gene Kelly*

Quiz 48
Question 12

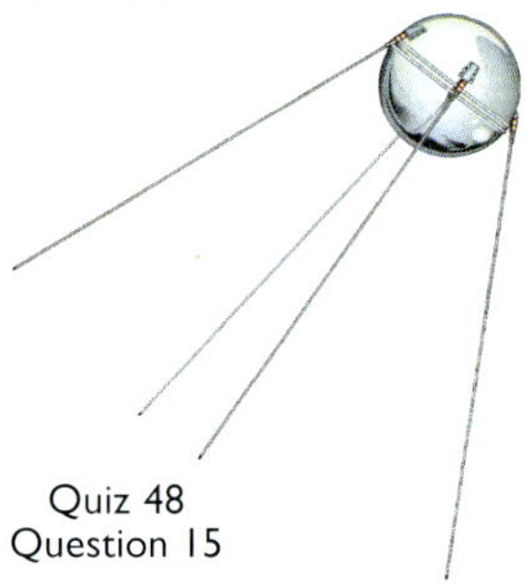

Quiz 48
Question 15

Quiz 48 Level 2

Questions		Answers
1	Which Asian people lived in tents called yurts?	*The Mongols*
2	Who invented the system of paying for postage with stamps?	*Rowland Hill*
3	Which 20th century Italian dictator was called 'Il Duce'?	*Benito Mussolini*
4	Which English poet wrote *The Iron Man*?	*Ted Hughes*
5	In which continent was the Empire of Mali?	*Africa*
6	What name did sailors give to the cape at the southern tip of Africa?	*The Cape of Good Hope*
7	What colour was the first artifical dye, discovered in 1855 by W.H. Perkin?	*Mauve*
8	Which two sides fought in the Battle of Crécy in 1346?	*English and French*
9	In what year did food rationing end – 1945, 1954 or 1966?	*1954*
10	Which instrument did the musician Paganini play?	*Violin*
11	What name is given to the peoples who first settled on the Pacific islands?	*Polynesians*
12	What was a 'Flying Fortress'?	*A World War II bombing plane*
13	Who led the allied troops at the Battle of El Alamein in 1942?	*Field Marshal Montgomery*
14	Who attacked US shipping at Pearl Harbor, Hawaii, in 1941?	*The Japanese*
15	What was the name of the first artificial satellite?	Sputnik

Quiz 47
Question 12

Quiz 47
Question 6

Quiz 49 Level 2

Questions		*Answers*
1	Who made the highest individual score ever in international Test cricket?	*Brian Lara (375)*
2	What fuel did Abraham Darby make in about 1709 by baking coal?	*Coke*
3	What kind of performance art is Marcel Marceau famous for?	*Mime*
4	Which religion was split by the 16th century Reformation?	*Christianity*
5	Where were playing cards invented?	*China*
6	Why were steam pumps needed in 18th century coal mines?	*To pump out water*
7	Which Hollywood actress began life as Norma Jean Baker?	*Marilyn Monroe*
8	Which Ethiopian leader was also known as Ras Tafari?	*Haile Selassie*
9	What huge stone shapes were found on Easter Island in the Pacific?	*Statues*
10	Which English king was held prisoner in Austria in 1193?	*Richard I*
11	What was the nickname of King Richard I of England?	*The Lionheart*
12	What were Zeppelin airships used for in the First World War?	*Bombing raids*
13	Which of the Beatles was born first?	*John Lennon*
14	Which country was named after the Rus tribe?	*Russia*
15	What was special about the space shuttle, launched in 1981?	*It can land and be re-used*

Quiz 50
Question 3

Quiz 50
Question 5

Quiz 50 Level 2

No.	Questions	Answers
1	What do Muslims call their pilgrimage to Mecca?	*The hajj*
2	What kind of machine was a 'mule', invented in 1779?	*A machine for spinning thread*
3	Who composed the *Young Person's Guide to the Orchestra*?	*Benjamin Britten*
4	Which sport made Babe Ruth famous?	*Baseball*
5	By what name is the Mongol leader Temujin better known?	*Genghis Khan*
6	Why were canal and railway construction workers called 'navvies'?	*It is short for 'navigators'*
7	How long did it take Marco Polo to reach China: 6 months, 2 years or 4 years?	*Four years*
8	What is the nickname of singer James Brown?	*The 'Godfather of Soul'*
9	Which country was ruled by Kenneth MacAlpin in the AD840s?	*Scotland*
10	Which part of Africa was known as 'the Land of Gold'?	*Ghana*
11	How do you spell the surname of the author of *Lord of the Rings*?	*Tolkien*
12	Which country did General Franco rule as dictator from 1939 to 1975?	*Spain*
13	Who built the Great Western Railway linking London and Bristol?	*I.K. Brunel*
14	What nationality was King Cnut of England?	*Danish*
15	What was the Leaning Tower of Pisa actually built as?	*A bell tower*

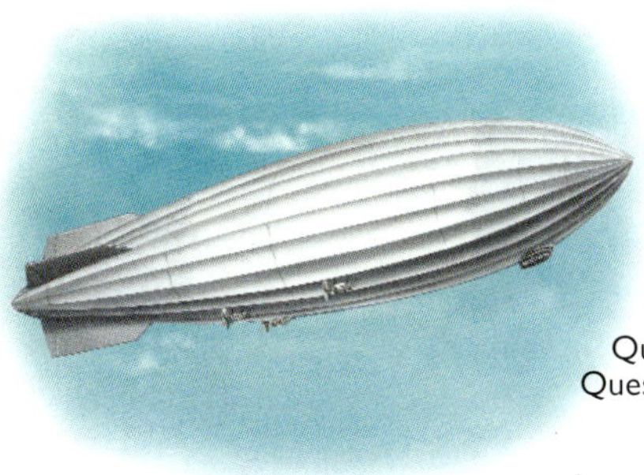

Quiz 49
Question 12

Quiz 49
Question 1

Quiz 51 Level 2

	Questions	Answers
1	Which two seas were linked by the Suez Canal in 1869?	*The Mediterranean and the Indian Ocean*
2	Which English poet was killed only a week before the First World War ended?	*Wilfred Owen*
3	Which Chicago gangster was nicknamed 'Scarface'?	*Al Capone*
4	Which two oceans were linked by the Panama Canal of 1914?	*The Pacific and the Atlantic*
5	Which people were scattered through the world in the diaspora?	*The Jews*
6	What kind of rocket launched the US Moon expedition in 1969?	A Saturn *rocket*
7	What, in degrees celsius, is absolute zero – 0°C, -273.16°C or -997.12°C?	*-273.16°C*
8	What shape was a lateen sail?	*Triangular*
9	Which king began the *Anglo-Saxon Chronicles* in AD891?	*Alfred the Great*
10	Why was the Pacific Ocean so called by early European sailors?	*Because it seemed to be 'peaceful'*
11	Which silent movie actor was known as the 'Great Lover'?	*Rudolph Valentino*
12	In which sport was Suzanne Lenglen a champion during the 1920s?	*Tennis*
13	What did Ernest Rutherford split for the first time in 1919?	*The atom*
14	What does the word apartheid mean?	*Apartness*
15	Where was the capital of the ancient Hebrew kingdom?	*Jerusalem*

Quiz 52 Question 11

Quiz 52 Level 2

Questions		Answers
1	Which Roman emperor founded Constantinople?	*Constantine*
2	What was the nickname of film comedian Joseph Francis Keaton?	*Buster*
3	Which country was led by the Ayatollah Khomeini?	*Iran*
4	Roughly how many hours would a factory hand have worked each day in the early 1800s?	*12-14*
5	What was the magical land created by C.S. Lewis in a series of books?	*Narnia*
6	What nationality was the poet Horace?	*Roman*
7	How many gospels are there in the Bible?	*Four*
8	Who was the first European to cross the Indian Ocean?	*Vasco da Gama*
9	What was the youngest age that anyone was allowed to work in Britain after 1819?	*Nine years old*
10	Who was Emperor of Japan during the Second World War?	*Hirohito*
11	The ancient Egyptian civilization evolved around which river?	*Nile*
12	How did John Warren make surgery less painful during the 1840s?	*He began to use anaesthetics*
13	Which major jazz composer and bandleader was known as 'Duke'?	*Edward Kennedy Ellington*
14	Which country did Britain and her allies fight against in the Crimean War?	*Russia*
15	Which volcano destroyed Pompeii in AD79?	*Vesuvius*

Quiz 51
Question 11

Quiz 51
Question 3

Quiz 53 Level 2

	Questions	Answers
1	What did doctors use leeches for?	*To suck excess blood from their patients*
2	Which director of suspense films always gave himself a walk-on part?	*Alfred Hitchcock*
3	Who was the last Chinese emperor?	*Pu-yi*
4	Who was the Roman god of wine?	*Bacchus*
5	Which Frenchman proved that diseases are spread by bacteria?	*Louis Pasteur*
6	What was the first aircraft to fly around the world without refuelling?	Voyager
7	In which part of the world did the Maya live?	*Central America*
8	What instrument was played by jazz musician Louis Armstrong?	*Trumpet*
9	What did the Luddites do in 1811?	*Smashed factory machines*
10	What did the Sioux Indians call their leather tents or dwellings?	*Tepees*
11	Which South American river did *Orellana* voyage down in 1542?	*The Amazon*
12	What do we call the war between England and France which lasted from 1337 to 1453?	*The Hundred Years' War*
13	Which American scientist proved in 1752 that lightning was an electric current?	*Benjamin Franklin*
14	How is William H. Bonney better known?	*Billy the Kid*
15	Who were the 'Forty-Niners'?	*Gold prospectors in the Californian rush*

Quiz 54
Question 14

Quiz 54
Question 6

Quiz 54 Level 2

	Questions	*Answers*
1	Which breakthrough in lighting was invented simultaneously by Edison and Swann in c.1860?	*The light bulb*
2	Which black athlete won four gold medals at the 1936 Berlin Olympics?	*Jesse Owens*
3	Which famous screen character was played by champion swimmer Johnny Weissmuller?	*Tarzan*
4	Where does the word 'holiday' come from?	*Medieval holy-day or feast day*
5	Which Indian prime minister was killed by her bodyguards in 1984?	*Indira Gandhi*
6	Who invented the telephone in 1876?	*Alexander Graham Bell*
7	What cartoon character was created by Georges Hergé?	*Tintin*
8	What kind of food was a medieval 'chewet'?	*A meat pie*
9	What kind of musical instrument was a tabor?	*A small drum*
10	Did Ernest Shackleton try to reach the North or the South Pole?	*South*
11	Which US president was known by his initials J.F.K?	*John F. Kennedy*
12	What was produced by a 'spinning jenny'?	*Cotton thread*
13	What was William Golding's first novel, published in 1953?	Lord of the Flies
14	What kind of material did a medieval mason work with?	*Stone*
15	What kind of food was 'pottage'?	*A thick lumpy soup*

Quiz 53
Question 8

Quiz 53
Question 5

Quiz 55 Level 2

	Questions	Answers
1	What was the job of a spinster in the Middle Ages?	*Spinning wool thread on a spindle*
2	What tricky job was performed by Eli Whitney's 1793 cotton gin?	*It removed seeds from cotton fibre*
3	What nationality is Pope John Paul II?	*Polish*
4	Who dreamed up *The Invisible Man* in 1897?	*H.G.Wells*
5	Which common tool is associated with the Swiss army?	*Swiss army knife*
6	Which Himalayan peak is named after the man who mapped the area?	*Everest*
7	What kind of popular music was pioneered by Scott Joplin?	*Ragtime*
8	In which year was the CD invented: 1959, 1979 or 1999?	*1979*
9	Which Italian city minted its own gold coins called 'florins'?	*Florence*
10	Which 'unsinkable' new liner sank in 1912 after hitting an iceberg?	*The* Titanic
11	What was Henry VIII's flagship which sank in 1545 and was raised again in 1982?	*The* Mary Rose
12	Who, in 1936, became the only British king to give up his throne voluntarily?	*Edward VIII*
13	Which planet did William Herschel discover in 1781?	*Uranus*
14	What unusual pet did Julius Caesar have?	*Giraffe*
15	What kind of weapon was a tomahawk?	*A hand axe*

Quiz 56
Question 7

Quiz 56
Question 13

Quiz 56 Level 2

Questions / *Answers*

	Questions	Answers
1	What does the word 'medieval' mean?	*'From the Middle Ages'*
2	Which element in the air was discovered by Lavoisier in the 1780s?	*Oxygen*
3	Which Russian composer caused a riot with his ultra-modern *Rite of Spring* in 1913?	*Igor Stravinsky*
4	What was a lord's 'demesne' in the Middle Ages?	*His land, or property*
5	Which country was crossed for the first time by Burke and Wills?	*Australia*
6	What is the largest public square in the world?	*Tiananmen Square*
7	What vegetable was struck by disease, causing Ireland's 'Great Hunger' after 1845?	*The potato*
8	What was the first full-length movie picture with sound, made in 1927?	The Jazz Singer
9	What was designed by Gustave Eiffel in 1889?	*The Eiffel Tower in Paris*
10	Which high explosive was invented by Alfred Nobel?	*Dynamite*
11	Groucho, Harpo and Chico belonged to which comic family group?	*The Marx brothers*
12	Which black US civil rights campaigner was assassinated in 1968?	*Martin Luther King*
13	Who rowed Bonnie Prince Charlie to safety in 1746?	*Flora Macdonald*
14	Who is the Buddhist leader of the Tibetan people?	*The Dalai Lama*
15	What was the most important weapon used by English and Welsh at Agincourt in 1415?	*The longbow*

Quiz 55
Question 15

Quiz 55
Question 5

Quiz 57 Level 2

	Questions	Answers
1	What were Scottish Highlanders banned from wearing in 1746?	*The kilt*
2	Which English actor became famous playing the monster in the 1935 film *Frankenstein*?	*Boris Karloff*
3	Who was the first person to reach the North Pole?	*Robert Peary*
4	What form of transport did Gottlieb Daimler help to pioneer?	*The motor car*
5	What was the Bastille in Paris, which was stormed by rebels in 1789?	*A prison*
6	Who was the first British monarch to be photographed?	*Queen Victoria*
7	Whose poems inspired the 1981 musical *Cats*?	*T.S. Eliot*
8	How many wives did King Henry VIII have?	*Six*
9	What did John Dunlop invent in 1887?	*Air-filled tyres*
10	Which comic actor made his name in the 1915 film *The Tramp*?	*Charlie Chaplin*
11	Who was the father of Queen Elizabeth I?	*Henry VIII*
12	Which English queen reigned for just nine days in 1553?	*Lady Jane Grey*
13	Which country was ruled by the Mogul emperor Akbar?	*India*
14	Which engineer produced the car called the Model-T?	*Henry Ford*
15	Who became Lord Protector of England in 1653?	*Oliver Cromwell*

Quiz 58
Question 1

Quiz 58
Question 3

Quiz 58 Level 2

Questions		*Answers*
1	Which English king was beheaded in 1649?	*Charles I*
2	How many sheep were there in Elizabethan Britain: 9,000, 1 million or 9 million?	*9 million*
3	Was Vaslav Nijinsky a) a composer b) a ballet dancer or c) a violinist?	*A ballet dancer*
4	Which Cornishman invented the first steam locomotive in 1803?	*Richard Trevithick*
5	What did the Gunpowder Plotters plan to blow up in 1605?	*The Houses of Parliament*
6	In which city was the skyscraper invented in 1885?	*Chicago*
7	Which Englishman kept a famous diary from 1660 to 1669?	*Samuel Pepys*
8	What nationality was Prince Henry the Navigator?	*Portuguese*
9	Who invented the 'Flying Shuttle' for weavers in 1733?	*John Kay*
10	Where was Dvorak when he composed his *New World* symphony?	*The USA*
11	Where did the ship *Mayflower* set out for in 1620?	*North America*
12	Which bay was the site of the first Australian settlement?	*Botany Bay*
13	When was the Great Fire of London?	*1666*
14	Of which country was Brian Boru the High King in about AD1000?	*Ireland*
15	Who was the oldest ever British monarch?	*Queen Victoria*

Quiz 57 Question 3

Quiz 57 Question 2

Quiz 59 Level 2

	Questions	Answers
1	What is the traditional symbol of the Welsh?	*A red dragon*
2	What shocking idea about astronomy was put forward by Copernicus in 1543?	*That the Earth goes round the Sun*
3	In which 19th-century novel does Long John Silver appear?	*R.L.Stevenson's* Treasure Island
4	Who was known as 'The Sun King'?	*Louis XIV of France*
5	What was the name of James Cook's ship on his first Pacific expedition?	*The* Endeavour
6	Which country was ruled by King William the Lion in the early 1200s?	*Scotland*
7	Who wrote the music used to accompany *Land of Hope and Glory?*	*Edward Elgar*
8	Who made a peaceful invasion of England and became king in 1688?	*William III*
9	Which animal is thought to have brought the Black Death into Britain?	*The black rat*
10	What farming machine did Jethro Tull invent?	*The seed drill*
11	Which peoples were led by Genghis Khan?	*The Mongols*
12	What were Celtic priests called?	*Druids*
13	Which fictional detective appears in *The Hound of the Baskervilles*?	*Sherlock Holmes*
14	What was produced in Bessemer's Converter of 1856?	*Steel*
15	What did the Nazis use as their symbol?	*The reversed swastika*

Quiz 60
Question 15

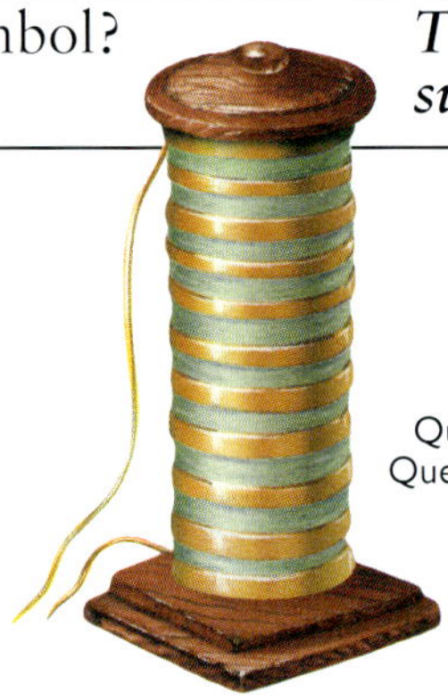

Quiz 60
Question 4

Quiz 60 Level 2

	Questions	Answers
1	Who founded the Methodist faith?	*John Wesley*
2	Which English author wrote *The Jungle Book* and the *Just So* Stories?	*Rudyard Kipling*
3	What was the surname of the English King Henry VII?	*Tudor*
4	Who invented the first chemical battery?	*Alessandro Volta*
5	What was the survey of all English property ordered by William the Conqueror?	*Domesday Book*
6	Which country was ruled by the empress Catherine the Great?	*Russia*
7	What disease attacked sailors because they had no fresh food?	*Scurvy*
8	Who wrote *The Rime of the Ancient Mariner*?	*Samuel Taylor Coleridge*
9	What was King John of England forced to sign in 1215?	*Magna Carta*
10	What were called doodlebugs in the Second World War?	*Flying bombs, or V-1s*
11	Which legendary British king had his court at Camelot?	*Arthur*
12	Which German brothers collected three famous volumes of fairy tales?	*Jacob and Wilhelm Grimm*
13	Who was the first president of the USA?	*George Washington*
14	What was kept in a medieval stew pond?	*Fish*
15	Which famous US pioneer paved the way for settlers in 1775?	*Daniel Boone*

Quiz 59
Question 9

Quiz 59
Question 1

Quiz 61 Level 2

Questions		*Answers*
1	Off which cape did Nelson defeat the French fleet in 1805?	*Cape Trafalgar*
2	What writing system was invented by Louis Braille in 1829?	*The use of raised letters for the blind*
3	Which classic horror story was written by a 21 year-old woman in 1818?	*Mary Shelley's* Frankenstein
4	What symbol did Crusader knights have on their banners?	*A red cross*
5	Which terrible trade did William Wilberforce help to abolish?	*Slave trade*
6	Which famous scientist sailed to South America on board the *Beagle*?	*Charles Darwin*
7	Which legendary monster lived in a labyrinth on Crete?	*The Minotaur*
8	Whose Eighth Symphony is known as *The Unfinished*?	*Schubert*
9	Who crowned Napoleon emperor of France in 1804?	*He crowned himself!*
10	What art, using small pieces of marble or glass, was used to decorate Roman villas?	*Mosaic*
11	What modern invention did John Logie Baird help to pioneer?	*The television*
12	In which war were tanks first used?	*World War I*
13	Which religion used a fish as its symbol?	*Christianity*
14	How did Russian poet Alexander Pushkin die in 1837?	*He was killed in a duel*
15	Was the Battle of Britain fought at sea or in the air?	*In the air*

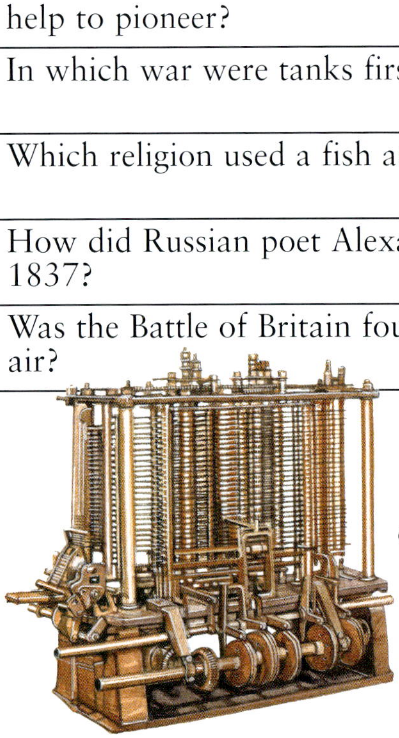

Quiz 62
Question 14

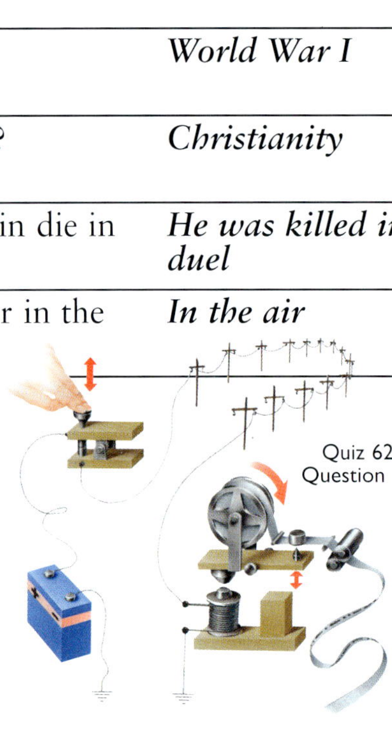

Quiz 62
Question 12

Quiz 62 Level 2

No.	Questions	Answers
1	Which Shawnee chief became a British Army officer in 1812?	*Tecumseh*
2	After which Norse god is the day Thursday named?	*Thor*
3	What was the name of Columbus's flagship in 1492?	Santa Maria
4	What new form of art was pioneered by W.H. Fox Talbot in the 1840s?	*Photography*
5	What was a penny black?	*A Victorian postage stamp*
6	In what year did the Allied landings in Normandy take place?	*1944*
7	Who led the Norman invasion of England in 1066?	*William of Normandy*
8	What was the giant tapestry which told the story of the Norman invasion of England?	*The Bayeux Tapestry*
9	Which British prime minister of the 19th century was also a best-selling novelist?	*Benjamin Disraeli*
10	Who led the British army at the Battle of Waterloo?	*The Duke of Wellington*
11	What do we call the European war which lasted from 1614 to 1648?	*The Thirty Years' War*
12	What kind of code, invented in 1837, was used for sending telegraph messages?	*Morse code*
13	Which Danish author wrote *The Snow Queen*?	*Hans Christian Andersen*
14	Who designed the world's first digital computer in 1835?	*Charles Babbage*
15	What religion were the Huguenots?	*Protestant*

Quiz 61
Question 11

Quiz 61
Question 7

Quiz 63 Level 2

	Questions	Answers
1	What breakfast food was invented by W.K. Kellogg in 1898?	*Corn flakes*
2	Who became King of the Zulus in 1816?	*Shaka*
3	Which writer created the characters of Scrooge, Mr Pickwick and Uriah Heep?	*Charles Dickens*
4	Which great palace was built by King Louis XIV of France?	*Versailles*
5	Why were the Roundheads so called?	*Because they cut their hair short*
6	In which American port did the famous 'Tea Party' protest take place in 1773?	*Boston*
7	In which country were chocolate bars invented?	*Switzerland*
8	Which German composer wrote the cycle of four operas called *The Ring*?	*Richard Wagner*
9	Which method of preserving food was made popular by Clarence Birdseye?	*Deep freezing*
10	Who was president of the USA during the Civil War?	*Abraham Lincoln*
11	When did the American colonies declare themselves independent of Britain?	*1776*
12	What machine was used to behead many people during the French Revolution?	*The guillotine*
13	Who formed a travelling circus he called 'the greatest show on earth'?	*P.T. Barnum*
14	How many of Magellan's men survived the round-the-world voyage?	*18 (out of 243)*
15	How many Brontë sisters were there?	*Three*

Quiz 64 Question 6

Quiz 64 Question 3

Quiz 64 Level 2

	Questions	Answers
1	In which year was Napoleon defeated at Waterloo?	*1815*
2	Who wrote the *Communist Manifesto*, with Friedrich Engels, in 1848?	*Karl Marx*
3	Who invented the safety lamp for miners in 1816?	*Humphry Davy*
4	Who or what is Moby Dick in Melville's novel?	*A white whale*
5	In which continent was the empire of Benin?	*Africa*
6	What do the carmaker's initials VW stand for?	*Volkswagen*
7	What vital new invention did Gutenberg develop in the 15th century?	*Printing with moveable type*
8	On which country was the first atomic bomb dropped in 1945?	*Japan*
9	Who was the longest reigning British queen in history?	*Victoria (1837-1901)*
10	Which country did the Valois dynasty rule?	*France*
11	Which nurse organized a hospital for British troops during the Crimean War?	*Florence Nightingale*
12	When did the first scooter appear: 1902, 1932 or 1992?	*1902*
13	In which Austrian city did the waltz first become popular?	*Vienna*
14	Which empire did Cortés destroy in 1521?	*Aztec*
15	What nickname did Europeans give to the Turkish sultan Suleyman?	*'The Magnificent'*

Quiz 63 Question 8

Quiz 63 Question 15

Quiz 65 Level 2

Questions		*Answers*
1	Who crossed Niagara Falls on a tightrope in 1859?	*Charles Blondin*
2	What was the name of the steam locomotive built by George Stephenson in 1829?	Rocket
3	Which nationality of people founded the Ottoman Empire?	*Turks*
4	Which storybook castaway did Daniel Defoe base on Alexander Selkirk?	*Robinson Crusoe*
5	In which country is El Cid a national hero?	*Spain*
6	By what name was writer Charles Lutwidge Dodgson better known?	*Lewis Carroll*
7	In which country did the Bullet Train start operating in 1964?	*Japan*
8	Are Jesuit priests Roman Catholic or Protestant?	*Roman Catholic*
9	Which country was invaded on D-Day in 1944?	*France*
10	What was the name of the invasion fleet sent by Spain against England in 1588?	*The Armada*
11	Who wrote about the adventures of Tom Sawyer and Huckleberry Finn?	*Mark Twain*
12	What did a knight aim to do in a joust?	*Knock his opponent off his horse*
13	In which country was the Boer War fought?	*South Africa*
14	What do we call the plague which killed one third of Europe's population in the 1340s?	*The Black Death*
15	Who created the sculpture called *The Thinker*?	*Rodin*

Quiz 66
Question 11

Quiz 66
Question 6

Quiz 66 Level 2

	Questions	Answers
1	In which city did the first underground railway open in 1863?	*London*
2	Who founded the Salvation Army?	*William Booth*
3	The Chinese kept secret their way of making a certain kind of material. What was it?	*Silk*
4	Which country had a dynasty of emperors called the Manchu?	*China*
5	Which Persian astronomer is best known for his poems, or 'Rubaiyat'?	*Omar Khayyám*
6	Which Native American princess saved the life of settler John Smith in 1606?	*Pocahontas*
7	Which Irishman set up shelters for over 50,000 homeless children?	*Thomas Barnardo*
8	Which country was once ruled by warlords called shoguns?	*Japan*
9	What kind of aircraft was the *Hindenburg*?	*An airship*
10	Who wrote the poem about Heaven and Hell called *The Divine Comedy*?	*Dante*
11	What was the nickname given to hunter and wild west showman William Cody?	*Buffalo Bill*
12	What was the hinged part at the front of a knight's helmet?	*The visor*
13	Which literary character was supposedly based on Vlad the Impaler?	*Dracula*
14	Which Indian river is holy to Hindus?	*The Ganges*
15	Which Australian state was named after explorer Abel Tasman?	*Tasmania*

Quiz 65 Question 7

Quiz 65 Question 4

Quiz 67 Level 2

	Questions	Answers
1	Which 15th-century Italian painter also designed flying machines?	*Leonardo da Vinci*
2	Which Australian outlaw used a home-made suit of armour?	*Ned Kelly*
3	Which brothers built the first successful powered aircraft in 1903?	*Orville and Wilbur Wright*
4	What were the rulers of Ancient Egypt called?	*Pharaohs*
5	In which country is the sculpture of the Sphinx?	*Egypt*
6	What was the name of Don Quixote's cunning servant?	*Sancho Panza*
7	Which modern country was the site of the ancient Indus Valley civilization?	*Pakistan*
8	What cause did Emmeline Pankhurst fight for?	*Votes for women in Britain*
9	Which continent did the potato come from?	*America*
10	Which US sharpshooter was nicknamed 'Little Sure Shot'?	*Annie Oakley*
11	What was the name of the first supersonic airliner?	*Concorde*
12	In which century were the first cannons invented: 10th, 14th or 17th?	*14th century*
13	Which diagram, drawn by Leonardo da Vinci, shows the proportions of man?	*Vitruvian man*
14	Which desert island, discovered by the Dutch, was home to the dodo?	*Mauritius*
15	What kind of vessel, first produced in 1959, is also known as an Air Cushion Vehicle?	*A hovercraft*

Quiz 68
Question 2

Quiz 68
Question 10

Quiz 68 Level 2

	Questions	Answers
1	How many crusades were there?	*Eight*
2	In which English town was William Shakespeare born?	*Stratford-upon-Avon*
3	Which great African river was explored by H.M. Stanley in 1889?	*The Congo*
4	Where was the 'Promised Land' of the ancient Israelites?	*Palestine*
5	Which steamship of 1843 was the first to cross the Atlantic using a screw propeller?	*The* Great Britain
6	In which country is Shinto one of the major religions?	*Japan*
7	Who was the last Tsar of Russia?	*Nicholas II*
8	Which two British aircraft played major parts in winning the Battle of Britain?	*Hurricane and Spitfire*
9	Who were the native people of New Zealand when Europeans first arrived?	*Maoris*
10	What revolutionary type of firearm was invented by Richard Gatling in 1862?	*The machine gun*
11	Apart from the horse, what large animal was used to pull early carts and ploughs?	*The ox*
12	Which 17th-century Dutch artist painted a famous series of self-portraits?	*Rembrandt*
13	Which Russian revolutionary leader changed his name to 'Man of Iron'?	*Lenin*
14	What kind of weapon was a Colt Peacemaker?	*A revolver*
15	Which of the Seven Wonders of the World was in Babylon?	*The Hanging Gardens*

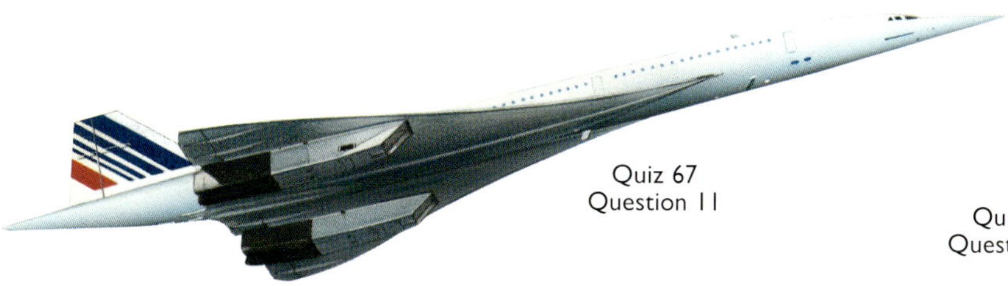

Quiz 67
Question 11

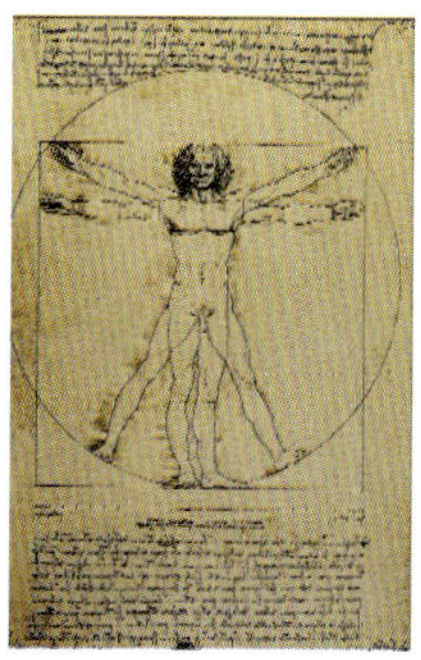

Quiz 67
Question 13

Quiz 69 Level 2

Questions		Answers
1	In which part of the world did farming begin: Australia, the Middle East, or North America?	*The Middle East*
2	Who was the first European to reach America after the Vikings?	*John Cabot*
3	What masterpiece did John Bunyan write in 1678, while in prison?	The Pilgrim's Progress
4	What was the name of the ruling council in Ancient Rome?	*The Senate*
5	What is the highest mountain in North America?	*Mt McKinley*
6	What was the name of the boat in which Drake sailed around the world?	*The* Golden Hind
7	Which island in San Francisco Bay was once used as a prison?	*Alcatraz*
8	In what shape are the stones of Stonehenge set out?	*A circle*
9	Who, in 1883, became the last Apache leader to surrender to the whites?	*Geronimo*
10	How many syllables are there in a haiku?	*17*
11	In what type of wagon did cowboys keep their possessions?	*Chuck wagon*
12	What was the surname of the man who invented the exploding shell in 1784?	*Shrapnel*
13	Why were iron weapons better than bronze ones?	*They were harder and stayed sharper*
14	Who were the rival sides in the English Wars of the Roses?	*Lancaster and York*
15	From which Italian town did St Francis come?	*Assisi*

Quiz 70
Question 9

Quiz 70
Question 14

Quiz 70 Level 2

	Questions	*Answers*
1	When did the first tank go into battle: 1815, 1916 or 1940?	*1916*
2	In Swift's *Gulliver's Travels*, what is the name of the land of giants?	*Brobdingnag*
3	In which year did the Spanish Armada try to invade England?	*1588*
4	Which king freed Scotland from English rule in 1314?	*Robert Bruce*
5	What was the name of John Cabot's boat?	The Matthew
6	In what state is Monument Valley?	*Utah*
7	Who was the first person to sail right round New Zealand?	*James Cook*
8	What do the composer J.S. Bach's initials stand for?	*Johann Sebastian*
9	Which aviator made the first solo flight across the Atlantic?	*Charles Lindbergh*
10	What name was given to the house on a Roman estate?	*Villa*
11	What was the name of Raleigh's first and unsuccessful colony in North America?	*Virginia*
12	Which German/English composer wrote *The Messiah*?	*Handel*
13	What was the average lifespan of a European peasant in 1300: 25, 45 or 65 years?	*25 years*
14	What kind of weapon is a bazooka?	*A hand-held rocket launcher*
15	What word for a castle prison do we get from the Norman 'donjon'?	*Dungeon*

Quiz 69
Question 11

Quiz 69
Question 6

Quiz 71 Level 2

	Questions	Answers
1	Which teenage girl led the French army to victory in 1429?	*Joan of Arc*
2	In Norse mythology, who was the most powerful of all the gods?	*Odin*
3	What was the profession of Thomas Chippendale (1718-1779)?	*Furniture maker*
4	What nationality was Christopher Columbus?	*Genoese (Italian)*
5	What technique was used by ranchers to identify their cattle?	*Cattle branding*
6	How was a Viking longship steered?	*With a long oar in the stern*
7	At what age did Mozart compose his first works?	*Five years old*
8	What was first exploded in New Mexico, USA in 1945?	*Atomic bomb*
9	In which country is the ancient burial ground known as 'The Valley of the Kings'?	*Egypt*
10	Which European travelled to China in the 1270s?	*Marco Polo*
11	Which poet addressed a mouse as 'wee, sleekit, cow'rin, tim'rous beastie'?	*Robert Burns*
12	What do the initials NATO stand for?	*North Atlantic Treaty Organization*
13	What kind of vehicle was a caravel?	*A sailing ship*
14	What is the short name for the system known as Radio Detection and Ranging?	*Radar*
15	In what year was Nelson Mandela released from prison?	*1990*

Quiz 72
Question 13

Quiz 72 Level 2

	Questions	*Answers*
1	What gorge, containing the Colorado River, reaches depths of over 1.7 km?	*Grand Canyon*
2	Where were the Spice Islands?	*The Moluccas, in the South China Seas*
3	Who was the founding father of the Sikh religion?	*Guru Nanak*
4	Who was the first Englishman to sail around the world?	*Francis Drake*
5	Which German composer wrote much of his greatest music after becoming deaf?	*Beethoven*
6	Which explorer gave his name to the strait between Asia and North America?	*Vitus Bering*
7	Which European people were the first to settle in Greenland?	*The Vikings*
8	What was produced on a ‘spinning jenny’?	*Cotton or wool thread*
9	What is special about the Hawker Harrier fighter plane of 1969?	*It could take off and land vertically*
10	Where did the Silk Road run?	*From China to the Mediterranean*
11	Which Spanish soldier conquered Peru in the 1530s?	*Francisco Pizarro*
12	Which leader reached the South Pole in 1912 but died on the return journey?	*Robert Falcon Scott*
13	What was a Sopwith Camel?	*A First World War fighter plane*
14	Which Spanish leader defeated the Aztec empire in Mexico?	*Hernando Cortés*
15	How many sets of wings does a biplane have?	*Two*

Quiz 71
Question 5

Quiz 71
Question 13

Quiz 73 Level 2

	Questions	Answers
1	Which lost Inca city was re-discovered by Hiram Bingham in 1911?	*Machu Picchu*
2	Which country was ruled by Ivan the Terrible?	*Russia*
3	Who was the first woman to fly solo across the Atlantic?	*Amelia Earhart*
4	Who wrote the poem *Jerusalem*?	*William Blake*
5	Which Norwegian adventurer sailed the Pacific on a balsawood raft?	*Thor Heyerdahl*
6	What was the name of the short arrow shot from a crossbow?	*A bolt, or 'quarrel'*
7	Which Scottish leader defeated the English at Bannockburn in 1314?	*Robert Bruce*
8	In the First World War, what was 'No Man's Land'?	*The area between the front-line trenches*
9	Which San Franciscan bridge was completed in 1937 and spans 1,280 m?	*Golden Gate Bridge*
10	Which Italian artist had the surname Buonarroti?	*Michelangelo*
11	How many soldiers did a Roman centurion command?	*100*
12	A Viking longship had two forms of power to push it along: a sail and - ?	*Oars*
13	How did the English King Harold die at the Battle of Hastings in 1066?	*He was shot in the eye by an arrow*
14	Who reached the summit of Everest with Edmund Hillary in 1953?	*Tensing Norgay*
15	What were the slits in castle walls used for?	*Shooting arrows through*

Quiz 74 Question 7

Quiz 74 Question 3

Quiz 74 Level 2

	Questions	Answers
1	Who was 77 years old when he made his second trip in space?	*John Glenn*
2	Which continent was named after the explorer Amerigo Vespucci?	*America*
3	Who wrote *The Canterbury Tales*?	*Geoffrey Chaucer*
4	Was Queen Mary I of England a Catholic or a Protestant?	*A Catholic*
5	What was Neil Armstrong the first person to do in 1969?	*Walk on the Moon*
6	What kind of siege weapon was a trebuchet?	*A giant sling shot*
7	Which empire was once ruled by Nero?	*Ancient Rome*
8	Who was the first American woman to travel in space?	*Sally Ride*
9	Who led the Turkish armies against the Christian forces in the Third Crusade?	*Saladin*
10	Altogether, how many soldiers fought at the Battle of Waterloo in 1815: 1,400, 14,000 or 140,000?	*140,000*
11	What nationality was the explorer Vasco da Gama?	*Portuguese*
12	Which part of the world was explored by Mungo Park?	*West Africa*
13	Which English king defeated the Danes in AD878?	*Alfred the Great*
14	Who led the first white expedition overland to the US west coast in 1804?	*Lewis and Clark*
15	What was the system of picture writing used in Ancient Egypt called?	*Hieroglyphics*

Quiz 73 Question 7

Quiz 73 Question 4

Quiz 75 Level 2

	Questions	*Answers*
1	What did Genghis Khan's name really mean?	*World Emperor*
2	Who was Labour Party leader before Tony Blair?	*John Smith*
3	Who was the first European to cross the Australian outback?	*Charles Sturt*
4	What was Jesus's home village?	*Nazareth*
5	In which two countries did the ancient Maya culture exist?	*Mexico and Guatemala*
6	At which London theatre were most of Shakespeare's greatest plays first performed?	*The Globe*
7	Who was H.M. Stanley sent to Africa to find in 1871?	*David Livingstone*
8	Of which country was Cleopatra the queen?	*Egypt*
9	Which royal house did both Edward I and Richard II belong to ?	*House of Plantagenet*
10	Which European country did Garibaldi fight to unite in 1860?	*Italy*
11	Which English explorer published a famous translation of the *Arabian Nights*?	*Richard Burton*
12	Which dynasty, famous for their vases, ruled China between 1368 and 1644?	*Ming*
13	In which century did Marco Polo visit China?	*13th century*
14	Where did Columbus actually land after crossing the Atlantic in 1492?	*The Bahamas*
15	What kind of bridge was first built in Coalbrookdale, Shropshire?	*An iron bridge*

Quiz 76
Question 8

Quiz 76
Question 10

Quiz 76 Level 2

Questions / *Answers*

	Questions	Answers
1	Who was the 'Young Pretender', who tried to seize the British throne in 1745?	*Bonnie Prince Charlie*
2	Which woman flew solo from England to Australia in 1930?	*Amy Johnson*
3	Which African river was explored by John Hanning Speke in the 1860s?	*The Nile*
4	Which part of the world was explored by Fridtjof Nansen?	*The Arctic*
5	Which nation provided reinforcements to the British at Waterloo?	*Prussia*
6	Early people used flints for two main purposes. One was to make tools. What was the other?	*To make fire*
7	Who was the second wife of King Henry VIII?	*Anne Boleyn*
8	Who was the first person to fly across the English Channel?	*Louis Blériot*
9	Which blind Greek poet is believed to have written *The Iliad* and *The Odyssey*?	*Homer*
10	Who led the first expedition to reach the South Pole?	*Amundsen*
11	In which English county is the site of the Battle of Edgehill?	*Warwickshire*
12	Would you have found a plesiosaur in the sea, in the air or on the ground?	*In the sea*
13	In which year did the Blitz on London start?	*1940*
14	Which space shuttle exploded in flight, killing all crew members?	Challenger
15	Who was the Welsh prince who led a revolt against English rule in 1400?	*Owain Glyn Dwr*

Quiz 75
Question 8

Quiz 75
Question 7

Quiz 77 Level 3

	Questions	Answers
1	Which continent did Mary Kingsley explore?	*Africa*
2	Which country did Germany invade in September 1939?	*Poland*
3	Who was the father of Britain's King Edward VII?	*Prince Albert (husband of Queen Victoria)*
4	Who was the first woman in space?	*Valentina Tereshkova (USSR, in 1963)*
5	With what invention is the name of Gillette associated?	*The safety razor*
6	The Northrop f-5 'Freedom fighter' saw service in which war: World War II or the Vietnam War?	*Vietnam War*
7	What was the name of the giant statue that once stood at the entrance of Rhodes harbour?	*The Colossus*
8	Which battle did King Harold of England win in 1066?	*Stamford Bridge, fighting Norwegians*
9	What do we call a picture carved from a flat stone, as were produced by ancient people?	*A relief*
10	What medical first did Christiaan Barnard of South Africa achieve in 1967?	*First heart transplant*
11	Which animals did armies in India and Cambodia use like tanks?	*Elephants*
12	In which city is there a famous opera house with sail-like roofs, opened in 1973?	*Sydney, Australia*
13	Samuel Pepys is remembered for writing what?	*His diary (1660 – 1669)*
14	To make a spark, what must flint be struck against?	*Iron*
15	In what sport was Joe Louis a world champion?	*Boxing*

Quiz 78
Question 11

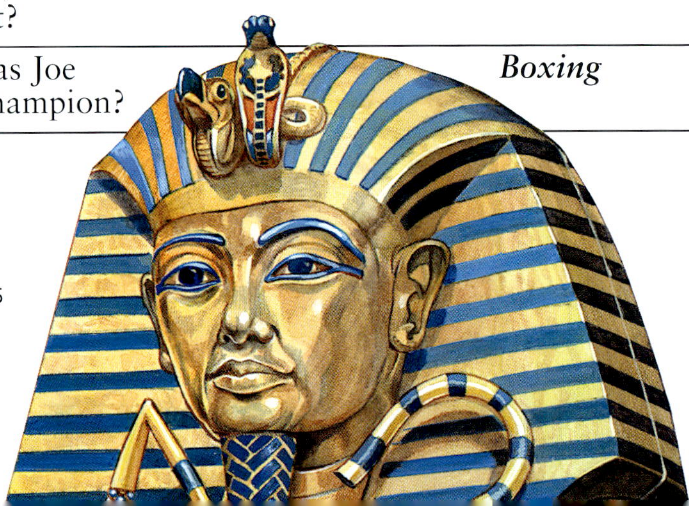

Quiz 78
Question 15

Quiz 78 Level 3

Questions			Answers
1		Where did Joshua Slocum sail from 1895 to 1898?	*Around the world (first person to do this alone)*
2		Which Greek hero could only be wounded in his heels?	*Achilles*
3		In which war was radar first used?	*World War II (1939-1945)*
4		What was the name of the Scottish hero in the film *Braveheart*?	*William Wallace*
5		In which Indian city did Mother Teresa do her good works?	*Calcutta*
6		Which Christian saint is famous for his love of animals?	*St Francis of Assisi (1182-1226)*
7		Who won the Six-Day War of 1967?	*Israel*
8		Which Tudor warship was raised from the seabed and is now preserved in Portsmouth, England?	*The* Mary Rose
9		Which land did Cartier claim for France in 1534?	*Canada*
10		In which story do Captain Nemo and the submarine *Nautilus* appear?	Twenty Thousand Leagues under the Sea
11		Which of King Henry VIII's wives was mother of Queen Elizabeth I?	*Anne Boleyn*
12		Was the Arab Ibn Battuta a famous traveller or a famous doctor?	*A famous traveller*
13		The artist Canaletto painted many views of which Italian city?	*Venice*
14		What word meaning 'sudden fear' is derived from the name of the Greek god Pan?	*Panic*
15		Which Egyptian pharaoh's tomb was discovered in 1922?	*Tutankhamun*

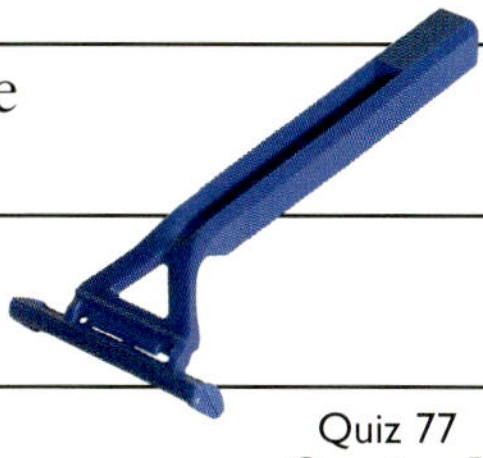

Quiz 77
Question 5

Quiz 77
Question 6

Quiz 79 Level 3

	Questions	Answers
1	What caused the death of the statesman and scientist Francis Bacon?	*He caught cold whilst freezing food in snow*
2	Which English king tried to make the tide obey him to show how powerless he was?	*King Canute*
3	What do we call the illustrations which Celtic monks used to adorn religious works?	*Illuminations*
4	What happened to the Japanese cities of Hiroshima and Nagasaki in August 1945?	*They were destroyed by atomic bombs*
5	Who led a revolution in Cuba in 1959?	*Fidel Castro*
6	Where is Dunkirk, from where over 300,000 service men were evacuated in World War Two?	*Northern France*
7	In which country was the medical treatment called acupuncture developed?	*China*
8	By what name was Martha Cannary better known in the Wild West?	*Calamity Jane*
9	What branch of mathematics did the ancient Egyptians develop when building the pyramids?	*Geometry*
10	Where is the North-West Passage, discovered in 1906 by Roald Amundsen?	*Around Canada. It links the Atlantic and Pacific*
11	The people of which country worshipped the gods Amun and Osiris: Mexico, Egypt or Greece?	*Egypt*
12	Which American frontiersman was killed at the Battle of the Alamo in 1836?	*Davy Crockett*
13	What kind of triangular sail invented in about AD500 allowed ships to sail more into the wind?	*The lateen sail*
14	Which ancient Indian religion strictly forbids its followers from harming any living thing?	*Jainism*
15	Who wrote the poem *The Charge of the Light Brigade*?	*Alfred Tennyson*

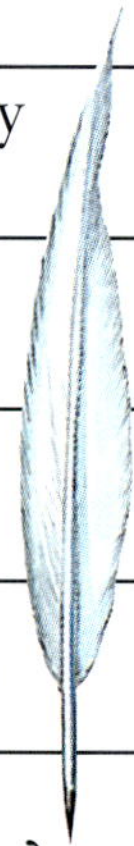

Quiz 80 Question 12

Quiz 80 Question 2

Quiz 80 Question 4

Quiz 80 Level 3

	Questions	*Answers*
1	Which US airman flew over both the North and South Poles?	*Richard E. Byrd*
2	Which king sent the Spanish Armada to war against England in 1588?	*Philip II*
3	By what name is the French king Charles the Great better known?	*Charlemagne*
4	What was a Dutchman named Hans Lippershey the first to look through in about 1600?	*The telescope*
5	What did Robert Bunsen invent?	*A gas burner (used in laboratories)*
6	When was the first airmail postal service introduced: 1911, 1921 or 1931?	*1911 (across London)*
7	What nationality was the composer Sibelius?	*Finnish*
8	Which calendar starts 3,760 years before the birth of Jesus Christ?	*The Jewish calendar*
9	Which US president was a famous general during World War II?	*Eisenhower*
10	What did Robert Watson-Watt invent in the 1930s?	*Radar*
11	What kind of armour did Norman knights wear?	*Chain-mail*
12	Before the invention of pens, what was a feather called when it was trimmed and used for writing?	*A quill*
13	Who was the first European to sail round the Cape of Good Hope?	*Bartolomeu Dias (Portugal)*
14	Which British poet died in Greece in 1824?	*Byron*
15	Which British king spoke German but hardly any English?	*George I*

Quiz 79
Question 11

Quiz 79
Question 3

Quiz 81 Level 3

#	Questions	Answers
1	What nationality was atom scientist Niels Bohr?	*Danish*
2	Which king ruled England, Denmark and Norway at the same time?	*Canute (or Cnut)*
3	Where was the great gold rush of 1849?	*California*
4	How many astronauts have stood on the Moon: two, eight or twelve?	*Twelve*
5	What crop did Jimmy Carter grow before he became US president?	*Peanuts*
6	After whom is the Bering Strait named?	*Danish explorer Vitus Bering*
7	Which two important metals were mined in England during Roman times?	*Lead and tin*
8	Which science-fiction story on radio caused a panic in the USA in 1938?	The War of the Worlds
9	In which Asian country was the Khmer empire founded in about AD900?	*Cambodia*
10	Which British prime minister had the forenames Margaret Hilda?	*Margaret Thatcher*
11	Did Mongol soldiers drink horse's milk, coffee, or pineapple juice?	*Horse's milk*
12	Was the first globe of the Earth made in 1350, 1492 or 1796?	*1492*
13	Which fireworks-styled weapons were first used in China?	*Rockets*
14	What were the pyramid-like platforms built in ancient Mesopotamia called?	*Ziggurats*
15	Which metal made Andrew Carnegie's millions?	*Steel*

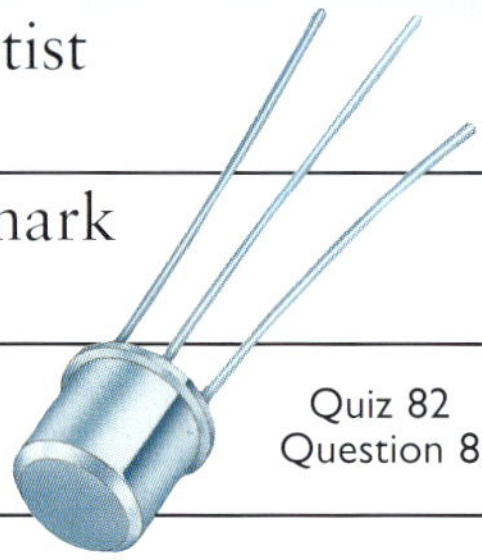

Quiz 82
Question 8

Quiz 82
Question 5

Quiz 82
Question 7

Quiz 82 Level 3

Questions		Answers
1	In which continent are the Atlas Mountains?	*Africa*
2	Michael Collins was a famous revolutionary: in which country?	*Ireland*
3	Is Verdi's *Nabucco* a disease, an opera, or a rare African bird?	*An opera*
4	Which country does Edam cheese come from?	*The Netherlands (Holland)*
5	What is the large medieval catapult that was used to attack castles called?	*Trebuchet*
6	Which Roman god was ruler of the Underworld?	*Pluto*
7	In which country did samurai warriors live?	*Japan*
8	Which 1947 invention made pocket-sized radios possible?	*The transistor*
9	A famous thriller writer wrote a children's book called *Chitty Chitty Bang Bang* – who was he?	*Ian Fleming*
10	Who won the sea battle of Sluys in 1346?	*The English (beating the French)*
11	In which Shakespeare play does a prince of Denmark see his father's ghost?	Hamlet
12	What year was the first digital computer built: 1930, 1946, or 1965?	*1946*
13	Which TV puppets worked for an organization called International Rescue?	*Thunderbirds*
14	Which oath, taken by modern doctors, is named after a Greek physician?	*The Hippocratic oath (after Hippocrates)*
15	How many kings of England have been called Henry?	*Eight*

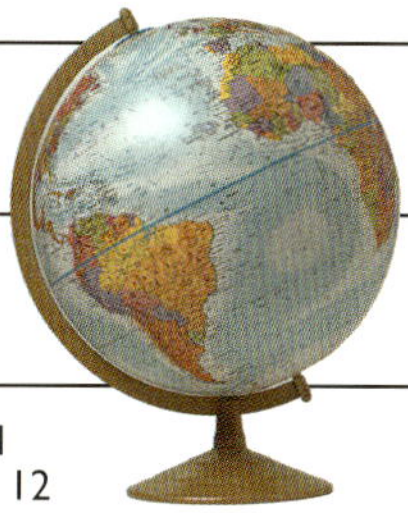

Quiz 81
Question 12

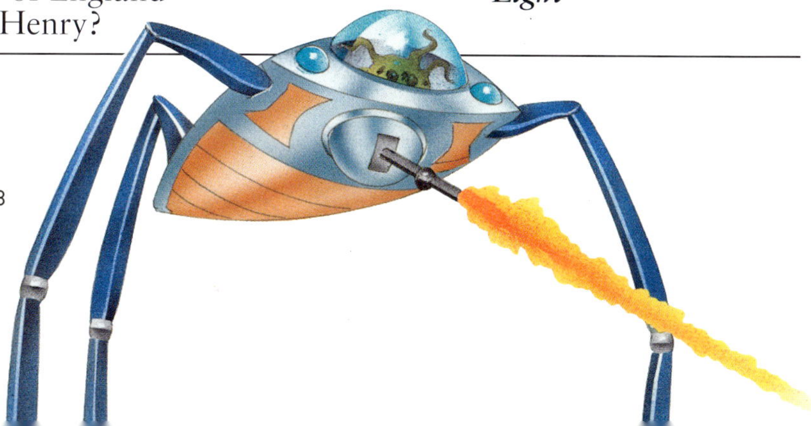

Quiz 81
Question 8

Quiz 83 Level 3

	Questions	*Answers*
1	Which US Army unit did Custer lead at the Little Big Horn?	*The 7th Cavalry*
2	Which real-life Tudor inspired a play and a film called *A Man for all Seasons*?	*Sir Thomas More*
3	Which river in Africa did 19th-century explorers strive to find the source of?	*The Nile*
4	Which bridge in London, completed in 1894, can open and close?	*Tower Bridge*
5	Which Israelite leader was ordered by God to kill his son Isaac?	*Abraham*
6	What prehistoric works of art were found in caves at Lascaux, France?	*Wall paintings*
7	What did Balboa see for the first time in 1513?	*The Pacific Ocean (first European to see it)*
8	Who made the first mass-produced car, the Model-T?	*Henry Ford*
9	Which number did the ancient Babylonians use as a unit for measuring time and angles?	*60*
10	Which islands was Magellan visiting when he was killed in a fight between rival tribes?	*The Philippines*
11	Was the *Turtle* of 1778 an early submarine, a primitive tank, or a rocket?	*An early submarine*
12	In 1971 East Pakistan became an independent country. What was it called?	*Bangladesh*
13	Which great Muslim leader made peace with the Crusaders in 1192?	*Saladin*
14	Which country was the first to introduce the metric system of weights and measures in 1795?	*France*
15	What emblem did a Crusader knight wear?	*A red cross*

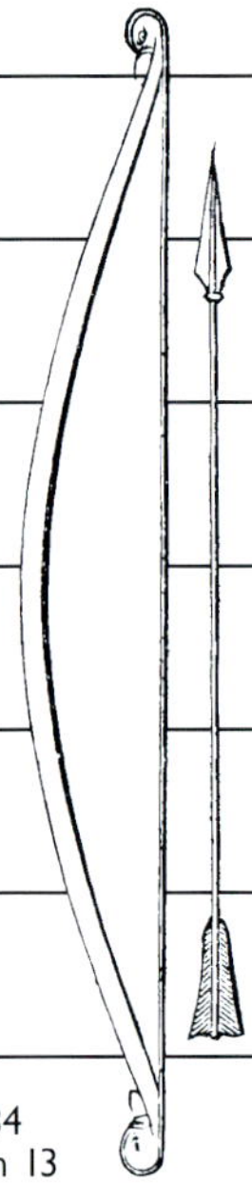

Quiz 84 Question 13

Quiz 84 Question 6

Quiz 84 Question 7

Quiz 84 Level 3

Questions		Answers
1	How many countries were founder members of the European Community in 1957?	*Six*
2	What was built across the United States in 1869?	*The first coast to coast railway*
3	Which mountains did Lewis and Clark lead an expedition across?	*The Rockies*
4	Which German composer, born in 1685, wrote *The Messiah* and the *Water Music*?	*Handel*
5	Who were supposed to obey the laws of chivalry?	*Medieval knights*
6	How many years ago did the first modern humans appear?	*150,000 years ago*
7	Which poet wrote *Kublai Khan*?	*Samuel Taylor Coleridge*
8	Who won the battle of Austerlitz in 1805?	*The French, led by Napoleon*
9	Which continent did Burke and Wills explore?	*Australia*
10	Which jazz musician was known as Satchmo?	*Louis Armstrong*
11	Which Greek city-state fought against Athens in the Peloponnesian war?	*Sparta*
12	Which ancient Greek hero led the expedition of the Argonauts?	*Jason*
13	Which could fire furthest: a longbow or a crossbow?	*A longbow*
14	Were Ginger Rogers and Fred Astaire a famous film dance team, comedians, or cartoon characters?	*A film dance team*
15	After which Greek god was the American manned Moon-landing spacecraft named?	*Apollo*

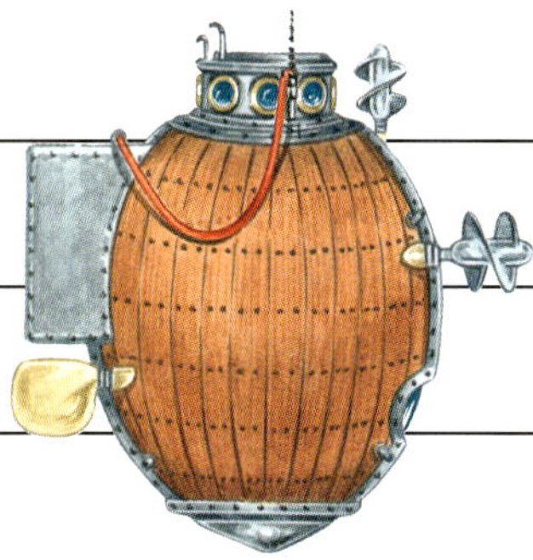
Quiz 83 Question 11

Quiz 83 Question 8

Quiz 83 Question 13

Quiz 85 Level 3

	Questions	Answers
1	In which country could you watch a kabuki play?	*Japan*
2	What was Thor Heyerdahl's boat *Ra* made from: reeds, ice, or oil drums?	*Reeds*
3	What was the very first kind of aircraft?	*A kite*
4	Which saint do we now call Santa Claus?	*St Nicholas*
5	When was the Great Fire of London?	*1666*
6	What did Vesalius study in the 1500s?	*Human anatomy – how the body worked*
7	Who was Jesse James?	*A famous outlaw*
8	The people of which country devised our modern numerals?	*India*
9	King Edward III of England had a famous warrior son: what was he called?	*The Black Prince*
10	What were the main weapons on Admiral Nelson's ship the *Victory*?	*Cannons*
11	What did Tycho Brahe of Denmark study?	*The stars*
12	What were Shermans and Grants in World War II?	*Tanks*
13	What invention of the early Middle Ages helped soldiers to fight on horseback?	*The stirrup*
14	What name did the Celts give to their poets?	*Bards*
15	Of which country was Jomo Kenyatta leader?	*Kenya*

Quiz 86
Question 11

Quiz 86
Question 1

Quiz 86 Level 3

	Questions	Answers
1	In what sort of boats did the Vikings travel?	*Longships*
2	Which American composer wrote *Rhapsody in Blue*?	*George Gershwin*
3	Which was invented first: the microscope or the telescope?	*The microscope*
4	Which civil rights leader was killed by James Earl Ray in 1968?	*Martin Luther King*
5	What oil-bearing substance did Noah use to coat the Ark and make it waterproof?	*Pitch*
6	Which Italian scientist is said to have dropped cannon balls from a tower to study how they fell to earth?	*Galileo Galilei*
7	How did the ancient Egyptians make casts to support broken limbs?	*With cloth strips soaked in mud*
8	True or false: knights sometimes wore helmets that they could see out of only by leaning forward?	*True: to protect their eyes while jousting*
9	Caliph Harun al-Rashid of Baghdad featured in which series of eastern stories?	The Arabian Nights
10	What is the most famous church designed by Sir Christopher Wren?	*St Paul's Cathedral*
11	In which war did the British first use grenades?	*World War II*
12	Who captured Constantinople in 1453?	*The Turks*
13	What kind of engine did the Greek engineer Hero design in the 1st century AD?	*A steam engine*
14	What name was given to religious images painted for the Byzantine church?	*Icons*
15	How did Blaise Pascal of France make addition faster in the 1640s?	*He made a mechanical calculator*

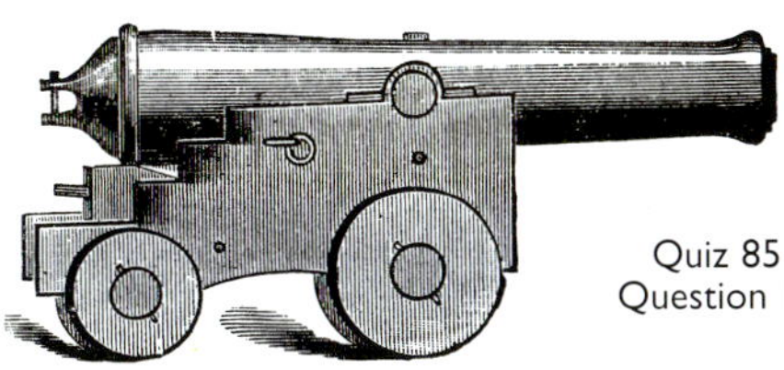

Quiz 85
Question 10

Quiz 85
Question 7

Quiz 87 Level 3

Questions / *Answers*

	Questions	Answers
1	Which English king signed Magna Carta?	*King John*
2	What law did Archimedes discover in the bath?	*Displacement*
3	Who wrote *Catcher in the Rye*?	*J.D. Salinger*
4	Which scientist published his 'laws of motion' in 1687?	*Isaac Newton*
5	Which Russian tsar worked in an English shipyard?	*Peter the Great*
6	Which King of Spain married Queen Mary of England?	*King Philip*
7	Which famous leader was nicknamed the 'little corporal'?	*Napoleon Bonaparte*
8	What kind of engine did Thomas Savery build in 1698?	*A steam pumping engine*
9	On which ship did the famous mutiny of 1789 happen?	*The* Bounty
10	What animals of the Spanish invaders frightened the Incas?	*Horses*
11	In which country was Adolf Hitler born?	*Austria*
12	Under what name did Samuel Langhorne Clemens become famous as a writer?	*Mark Twain*
13	In which country did Owen Glendower lead a revolt in 1400?	*Wales*
14	Did Jethro Tull make improvements in farming or medicine?	*Farming*
15	How many horses did the Egyptians normally use to pull their battle chariots?	*Two*

Quiz 88 Question 7

Quiz 88 Question 2

Quiz 88 Question 8

Quiz 88 Level 3

Questions / *Answers*

	Questions	Answers
1	In 1781 William Herschel spotted a planet: which one?	*Uranus*
2	Which English writer wrote a famous *Dictionary of the English Language?*	*Samuel Johnson*
3	What happened to the MP Spencer Perceval in 1812?	*He was assassinated*
4	When was the wheel invented: 32000BC, 3200BC or 320BC?	*3200BC in Sumeria*
5	Of which people was William Tell a national hero?	*The Swiss*
6	How many planets were known before a new one was discovered in 1781?	*Six had been known since ancient times*
7	How many legionaires were there in a *century*?	*Eighty*
8	Which country had a ruler called Ivan the Terrible?	*Russia*
9	What fabric did Wallace Carothers invent?	*Nylon*
10	Was Peter Paul Rubens a famous painter, poet, or dancer?	*Painter (1577-1640)*
11	Which Greek inventor discovered the laws of levers and pulleys?	*Archimedes*
12	In which country did warriors called shoguns rule?	*Japan*
13	In what year was Archduke Franz Ferdinand of Austria assassinated?	*1914*
14	Which country had the first steam railway?	*Britain (1825)*
15	How old was Mozart when he made his first tour as a performer?	*Six*

Quiz 87
Question 15

Quiz 89 Level 3

	Questions	Answers
1	What did Thomas Chippendale make?	*Furniture*
2	Was the battle of Lepanto in 1471 fought at sea or on land?	*At sea*
3	Against which disease did Edward Jenner pioneer vaccination in 1796?	*Smallpox*
4	Which US president resigned over the Watergate affair?	*Richard Nixon*
5	Who wrote the World War I war poem 'Dulce et Decorum Est'?	*Wilfred Owen*
6	Whose army are the Russians fighting in Tolstoy's novel *War and Peace?*	*The French army of Napoleon*
7	What year was the Persian Gulf War – 1980, 1985, or 1991?	*1991*
8	What was the name of the first genetically cloned mammal, a sheep?	*Dolly*
9	What is the first name of Queen Elizabeth II's sister?	*Margaret*
10	What opened between Paddington and Farringdon Street, London in 1863?	*The first underground railway*
11	Which king was put on the throne after the 'Glorious Revolution' in 1688?	*William of Orange*
12	From which countries did the Vikings begin their raids around northern Europe?	*Sweden, Norway Finland, Denmark*
13	Which three weapons were first used during World War I (1914-1918)?	*Aeroplanes, tanks and submarines*
14	Who started building the Tower of London in 1078?	*William the Conqueror*
15	Which English poet wrote a famous poem about daffodils?	*William Wordsworth*

Quiz 90
Question 3

Quiz 90 Level 3

Questions		*Answers*
1	In which century were machine guns invented?	*19th century*
2	In the 1800s Joseph Henry and Michael Faraday separately made a discovery about magnets: what?	*That a magnet has an electrical effect*
3	In a medieval motte and bailey castle, was the motte a mound or a ditch?	*A mound*
4	In which century were the first aerial bombs used?	*19th century, hung from Austrian balloons*
5	What was a 'nilometer' used for in ancient Egypt?	*To measure the depth of the River Nile*
6	What is the name of the hill near Jerusalem where Jesus was crucified?	*Calvary*
7	Who wrote *Gulliver's Travels?*	*Jonathan Swift*
8	Which British prime minister was born in Edinburgh in 1953?	*Tony Blair*
9	What killed the Greek playwright Aeschylus?	*A stone dropped by an eagle*
10	What was the favourite weapon of the Mongols?	*Bow and arrow*
11	Who ruled the Soviet Union from 1924 to 1953?	*Stalin*
12	Carib Indians thought Spanish explorers wore tortoise shells: what were the shells?	*Steel armour breastplates*
13	Who was the first Roman emperor to become a Christian?	*Constantine*
14	Who wrote the epic poem *Paradise Lost?*	*John Milton*
15	Which scientist discovered oxygen?	*Joseph Priestley*

Quiz 89 Question 1

Quiz 89 Question 12

Quiz 91 Level 3

Questions		Answers
1	Which country was led by a man who called himself Marshal Tito?	*Yugoslavia*
2	What was the Pyroscaphe of 1783?	*The first steam-driven boat*
3	In which year was the integrated circuit invented: 1959, 1969 or 1979?	*1959*
4	Idi Amin expelled 40,000 British Asians from which country?	*Uganda*
5	Which English king is known as 'the Unready'?	*Ethelred*
6	Which US president was assassinated in Dallas in 1963?	*John F. Kennedy*
7	From which Celtic tribe did Boudicca come?	*The Iceni*
8	Which English king led his army to victory at Agincourt?	*Henry V*
9	What Chinese invention of about 1400BC revolutionized the making of clay pots?	*The potter's wheel*
10	On which mountain is Noah's Ark believed to have come to rest?	*Mount Ararat, in modern Turkey*
11	What transport device did William Henson dream up in 1843?	*An aerial steam carriage but it never flew*
12	Did a concentric castle have one wall or more than one?	*More than one*
13	What was the first supersonic airliner, which entered service in 1976?	*Concorde*
14	Which ancient people discovered the principle of perspective in art?	*The Romans*
15	Which giant birds once roamed New Zealand?	*Moas*

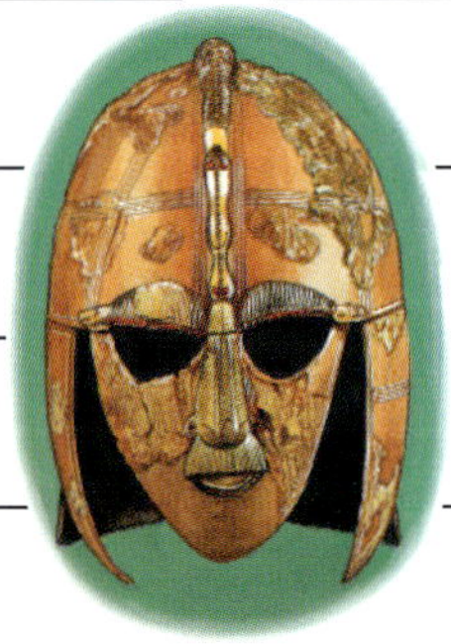

Quiz 92 Question 3

Quiz 92 Question 5

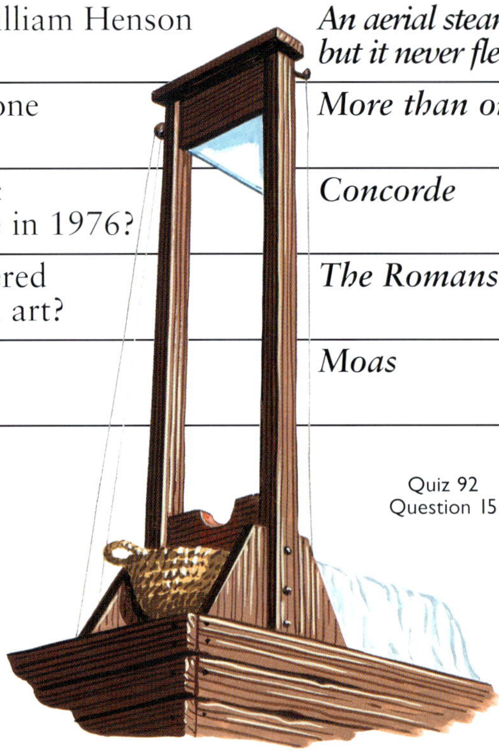

Quiz 92 Question 15

Quiz 92 Level 3

Questions / *Answers*

	Questions	Answers
1	What record did the Bell X-1 set in 1947?	*First supersonic flight by a piloted aircraft*
2	In which country was the war of the Three Henrys fought?	*France, in 1585*
3	What was one of the main finds at the Sutton Hoo burial ground?	*An ancient battle helmet*
4	What year did the Berlin Wall come down?	*1981*
5	On which planet did the *Viking 1* probe land in 1976?	*Mars*
6	Who wrote the first draft of the US Constitution: Jefferson, Lincoln, or Grant?	*Jefferson*
7	Which early central American people built pyramids and invented a calendar?	*The Maya*
8	Who was the first man to fly at Mach 1, the speed of sound at sea level?	*Charles Yeager*
9	In which century did soldiers start wearing grey or khaki uniforms?	*19th century*
10	Which great Islamic monument was built in Jerusalem in AD691?	*The Dome of the Rock*
11	Which beautiful woman was stolen from her husband and caused the Trojan war?	*Helen of Troy*
12	Which country's army was led by Gustavus Adolphus in the 1600s?	*Sweden*
13	Where did *Columbia* go in 1981?	*Into space; it was the first US space shuttle*
14	What form of propulsion did Frank Whittle pioneer?	*Jet propulsion*
15	How did France's Queen Marie Antoinette die?	*She was executed by guillotine*

Quiz 91
Question 8

Quiz 91
Question 7

Quiz 93 Level 3

Questions		*Answers*
1	What was President Lincoln doing when he was shot in 1865?	*Watching a play*
2	What was the name of the rocket that sent the Apollo spacecraft to the Moon?	Saturn 5
3	Which bloodthirsty Roman emperor was nicknamed 'Little Boots'?	*Caligula*
4	Who was the Norse god of thunder?	*Thor*
5	How many perfect numbers are known: 2, 12, 100, 1000?	*12*
6	Which 1950s singer sang with *The Crickets*?	*Buddy Holly*
7	What did Alexander Graham Bell invent in 1876?	*The telephone*
8	What does the word 'dinosaur' actually mean?	*It is Greek for 'terrible lizard'*
9	What was the family name of Diana, Princess of Wales?	*Spencer*
10	In which 18th-century war did Prussia fight France, Austria and Russia?	*Seven Years' War*
11	What happened to the American passenger pigeon early in the 20th century?	*It became extinct*
12	In which year did the prophet Muhammad flee from Mecca to Medina?	*622*
13	Was the Turbinia of 1897 a steam-turbine ship or a kind of airship?	*A steam-turbine ship*
14	Which country was ruled by the Shang dynasty?	*China*
15	When was the first hovercraft built: 1939, 1949 or 1959?	*1959*

Quiz 94
Question 3

Quiz 94
Question 10

Quiz 94 Level 3

	Questions	Answers
1	Which country set up the first national park?	*The USA (Yellowstone, 1872)*
2	In which city were the Beatles born?	*Liverpool*
3	Who commanded the Confederate forces in the American Civil War?	*General Robert E. Lee*
4	After whom is the orbital Space Telescope named?	*Edwin Hubble*
5	Which English general won the battle of Blenheim?	*Marlborough*
6	Which big cat lives in the cold mountains of Asia?	*The snow leopard*
7	Who was the patron goddess of Athens?	*Athene*
8	Who was it that gave a speech beginning "I have a dream"?	*Martin Luther King*
9	In which decade were talking films introduced?	*The 1920s*
10	Which war was fought between 1861 and 1865?	*The American Civil War*
11	Which countries were joined politically in 1707?	*England and Scotland*
12	Which Shakespeare play is about a Scottish king's murder?	Macbeth
13	In which country were cars first mass-produced in factories?	*USA*
14	What, in ancient Greece, was an amphora?	*A two-handled vase*
15	In what year did Fleming discover penicillin?	*1928*

Quiz 93 Question 14

Quiz 93 Question 7

Quiz 93 Question 8

Quiz 95 Level 3

	Questions	Answers
1	When did nuclear power plants start to generate electricity: 1930s or 1950s?	*1950s*
2	When was the first revolver made?	*1835*
3	What was different about sending a letter after 1840?	*Postage stamps were used for the first time*
4	Who was Ned Kelly?	*An Australian outlaw in the 1800s*
5	What were the small, hairy creatures that were the heroes in *The Lord of the Rings*?	*Hobbits*
6	In what year did William Shakespeare die: 1606, 1616 or 1626?	*1616*
7	Which human body part was the first to be successfully transplanted in 1954?	*The kidney*
8	In which century did people first use handkerchiefs?	*The 16th century*
9	Which Swedish tennis player won 5 Wimbledon men's singles titles in a row (1976 to 1980)?	*Bjorn Borg*
10	What were the *Merrimack* and *Monitor* ?	*The first armoured ships to fight*
11	What did Alice go through to get to Wonderland?	*A rabbit's burrow*
12	Which construction, the first to be built entirely of iron, was made in Coalbrookdale, England?	*An iron bridge*
13	Which president ordered the dropping of the first atomic bomb on Japan?	*Harry S. Truman*
14	For which English soccer club did Bobby Charlton play?	*Manchester United*
15	Which decade of the 20th century was known as The Jazz Age?	*The 1920s*

Quiz 96
Question 1

Quiz 96 Level 3

	Questions	*Answers*
1	What do we call the jagged tops of castle walls, through which archers could fire?	*Crenellations*
2	Which part of China passed from British rule in 1997?	*Hong Kong*
3	What did a man named Gatling invent in 1863?	*A rapid-firing gun (the first machine-gun)*
4	How did Sir John Franklin meet his death in 1847?	*He and his men were trapped in Arctic ice*
5	What subjects were early Islamic artists forbidden to paint?	*Animals and plants*
6	What kind of weapon was a Lee Enfield?	*A rifle*
7	What is the first book in the Bible?	*Genesis*
8	Which famous ship, which sank in 1912 on its first voyage, featured in a blockbuster movie?	*The* Titanic
9	Which natural wonder did Cook explore off eastern Australia?	*The Great Barrier Reef*
10	Which great Roman leader and general wrote an account of his campaigns in Gaul?	*Julius Caesar*
11	What did the steamship *Savannah* cross in 1819?	*The Atlantic Ocean*
12	In what language was the poem *Beowulf* written?	*Anglo-Saxon (or old English)*
13	Who was called the 'Liberator' of South America?	*Simón Bolívar*
14	Which sea route did Amundsen navigate in 1903-1906?	*The North-West Passage*
15	Which land was explored by the Viking Erik the Red in about 982?	*Greenland*

Quiz 95
Question 4

Quiz 95
Question 12

Quiz 97 Level 3

	Questions	Answers
1	Where was the world's biggest expanse of prairie?	*North America (before 1900)*
2	Which Egyptian queen was the lover of the Roman Mark Antony?	*Cleopatra*
3	In which country was the 1916 Easter Rising?	*Ireland*
4	Where was the battle of Dien Bien Phu fought in 1954?	*Vietnam*
5	What strong but delicate kind of ceramic was invented in China in about AD700?	*Porcelain*
6	Settlers in the Wild West tamed mustangs: what were mustangs?	*Wild horses*
7	What do we call poetry that is memorized and recited but not written down?	*Oral poetry*
8	Manet and Monet were both famous French . . . what?	*Painters*
9	What was the first name of the Mongol leader Khan, grandfather of Kublai Khan?	*Genghis*
10	What was the date of the D-Day invasion during World War II?	*June 6, 1944*
11	What was a prairie schooner?	*A covered wagon used by Western pioneers*
12	Who was British prime minister before Margaret Thatcher?	*James Callaghan*
13	Which American poet wrote *Leaves of Grass?*	*Walt Whitman*
14	Who commanded television's first starship *Enterprise*?	*Captain James Kirk*
15	Which two Russian cities endured long sieges during World War II?	*Leningrad and Stalingrad*

Quiz 98
Question 12

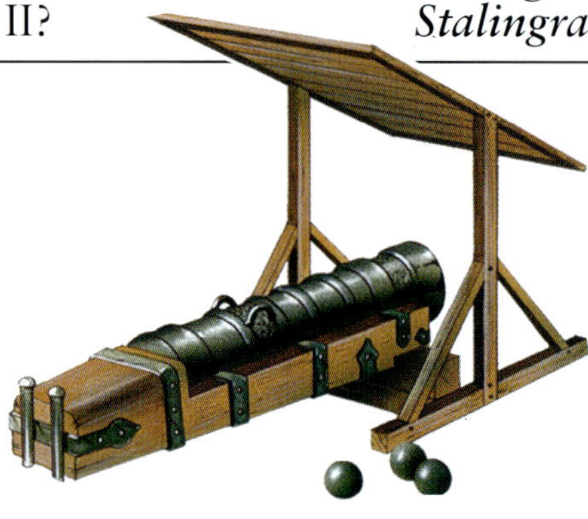

Quiz 98
Question 15

Quiz 98 Level 3

	Questions	*Answers*
1	Who invented the lightning conductor in June 1752?	*Benjamin Franklin*
2	From which country did Admiral Cheng Ho lead voyages of discovery?	*China*
3	Which river features in the title of a famous waltz tune by Strauss?	*The Danube (The Blue Danube)*
4	Which invader won a battle at Panipat in India in 1526?	*Babur*
5	Which great African empire was founded in about AD750?	*Ghana*
6	Luther Burbank was born in America in 1849: did he grow plants, fight battles, or write songs?	*He grew (and studied) plants*
7	Who first believed that the earth was round: the ancient Greeks, the Vikings or Columbus?	*The ancient Greeks*
8	Which ancient city did the archaeologist Heinrich Schliemann dig for?	*Troy*
9	By what name is Siddhartha Gautama better-known?	*Buddha*
10	Hosni Mubarak became president of which African country in 1981?	*Egypt*
11	Which country did Konrad Adenauer lead from 1949 to 1963?	*West Germany*
12	The ancient cities of Mohenjo Daro and Harappa were in which country?	*India*
13	A Roman city buried by a volcano in AD79 was rediscovered in the 1700s: what was its name?	*Pompeii*
14	What job did John Adams take on in 1796?	*President of the USA*
15	What was a bombard, invented in about 1340?	*An early cannon*

Quiz 97
Question 11

Quiz 99 Level 3

Questions		Answers
1	In *Peter Pan*, what is the name of the villainous pirate captain?	*Captain Hook*
2	What were searchlights used for in World War II?	*To pick out enemy bombers at night*
3	Which French female soldier was burnt to death in 1431 by the English?	*Joan of Arc*
4	Who was the most famous British scientist of the Middle Ages?	*Roger Bacon (about 1220-1292)*
5	Who succeeded Winston Churchill as British prime minister in 1945?	*Clement Attlee*
6	On which Pacific islands, visited by Darwin between 1831 and 1836 do giant tortoises live?	*The Galapagos*
7	Which record was broken by Donald Campbell in the *Bluebird* on September 19, 1956?	*The water speed record (286mph)*
8	What did the ancient Greeks call the Straits of Gibraltar, leading to the Atlantic?	*The Pillars of Hercules*
9	In which country was Kit Carson an explorer and trail-blazer?	*The USA*
10	What was the last play written by William Shakespeare?	*The* Tempest
11	In which war was the battle of Naseby?	*English Civil War*
12	What was cuneiform?	*The earliest kind of writing*
13	What did John Bardeen, William Shockley and Walter Brattain invent in the 1940s?	*The integrated circuit, or microchip*
14	Which engineer built the steamships *Great Britain* and *Great Eastern*?	*Isambard Kingdom Brunel*
15	Which European country invaded Abyssinia (Ethiopia) in the 1930s?	*Italy*

Quiz 100
Question 9

Quiz 100 Level 3

	Questions	*Answers*
1	Was Elvis Presley the singer's real name?	*Yes*
2	Who wrote *Pilgrim's Progress* ?	*John Bunyan*
3	Which queen was the subject of a film called *Mrs Brown*?	*Queen Victoria*
4	Which comet did the *Giotto* space probe whizz past in 1986?	*Halley's Comet*
5	Who painted *The Laughing Cavalier?*	*Frans Hals*
6	Nineveh and Assur were the chief cities of which empire?	*Assyrian*
7	The Silk Road ran between Europe and which country?	*China*
8	On which Mediterranean island did the mythical monster the Minotaur live?	*Crete*
9	What was the *Rocket*, built by Robert Stephenson in 1829?	*A steam engine*
10	Who said, "Never has so much been owed by so many to so few"?	*Winston Churchill (on the Battle of Britain)*
11	What was Enrico Caruso's claim to fame: singing, motor racing, or soccer?	*Singing*
12	What flew around the world in 1957?	Sputnik 1, *the first artificial satellite*
13	Who led the British to victory at Quebec in 1759?	*Wolfe*
14	What country produced the writers W.B. Yeats and Sean O'Casey?	*Ireland*
15	When was Bakelite, the first artificial plastic, invented: 1879, 1909 or 1939?	*1909*

Quiz 99 Question 3

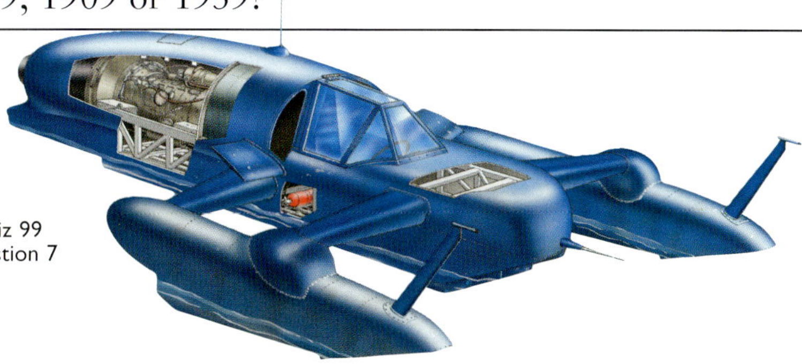

Quiz 99 Question 7

Quiz 101 Level 3

	Questions	Answers
1	What nationality was the painter John Constable?	*English*
2	Who drew up the first periodic table of the chemical elements in the 1860s?	*Dmitri Mendeleyev*
3	Which artist/writer created a cartoon Father Christmas and a snowman?	*Raymond Briggs*
4	In which year did Captain Cook begin the first of his round the world voyages: 1668, 1768 or 1868?	*1768*
5	In which country are there teachers of flower arranging called Flower Masters?	*Japan*
6	Whom did the USA fight in the war of 1812?	*Britain*
7	What musical instrument was Chopin famous for playing?	*Piano*
8	What was *Skylab*?	*The first US manned space station (1973-9)*
9	In 1896 the speed limit in Britain was raised . . . to what?	*12 mph*
10	Where did Roald Amundsen, who beat Captain Scott to the South Pole, come from?	*Norway*
11	Which country's army won the battle of Sedan in 1870?	*Germany (defeating France)*
12	From which ancient language do we get the word 'politics'?	*Greek*
13	Which nation did the Greek defeat after a long war in 479BC?	*The Persians*
14	What is a dagger with a very fine, slender blade called?	*A stiletto*
15	In 1897 it was discovered that which insect causes malaria?	*Mosquito*

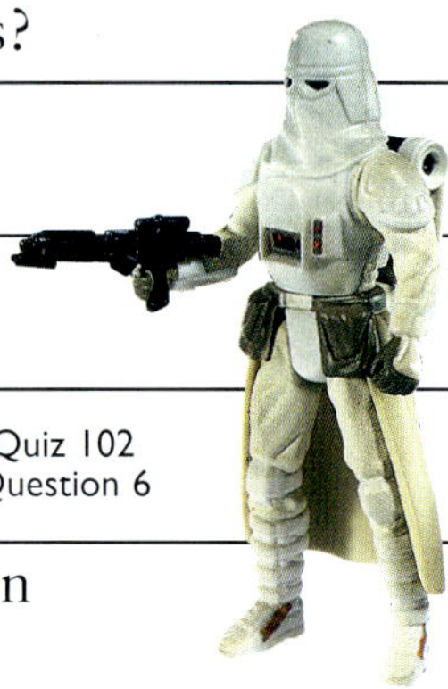

Quiz 102 Question 6

Quiz 102 Question 5

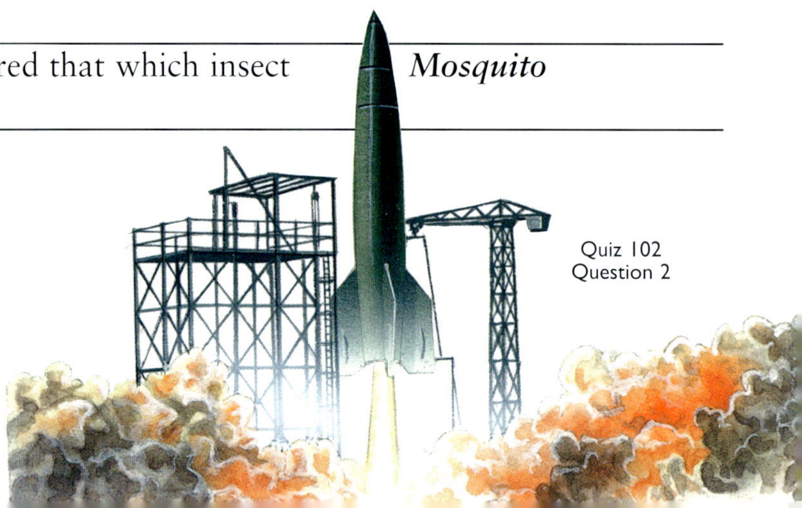

Quiz 102 Question 2

Quiz 102 Level 3

	Questions	Answers
1	In which sport was Knut Rockne a famous coach: American football, boxing, or cricket?	*American football*
2	What was a V-2?	*A German rocket of World War II*
3	What was the world land speed record in 1906: 78 mph, 98 mph or 128mph?	*128 mph*
4	Old maps show *Terra Australis Incognita* – what did this mean?	*Unknown Southern Continent, in Latin*
5	Who was made Lord Protector, and ruled England after the Civil War?	*Oliver Cromwell*
6	In which film series, started in 1977, do C-3PO and R2-D2 appear?	Star Wars
7	Which war was called 'the war to end all wars'?	*World War I (1914-1918)*
8	When did Russians begin exploring Siberia: 1500s, 1800s or 1900s?	*1500s*
9	Soldiers from which country were able to form a defensive 'tortoise' with their shields?	*Rome*
10	In 1710 the first model was built that showed how the planets moved. What was it called?	*An orrery*
11	In which country is the Muslim holy city of Mecca?	*Saudi Arabia*
12	The Library of Congress was founded in 1800 in which country?	*The USA*
13	Where did Robert Clive find fame and fortune in the 1700s?	*India*
14	What kind of races took place in the Circus Maximus in Rome?	*Chariot races*
15	Which planet was visited by the *Galileo* probe in 1995?	*Jupiter*

Quiz 101
Question 7

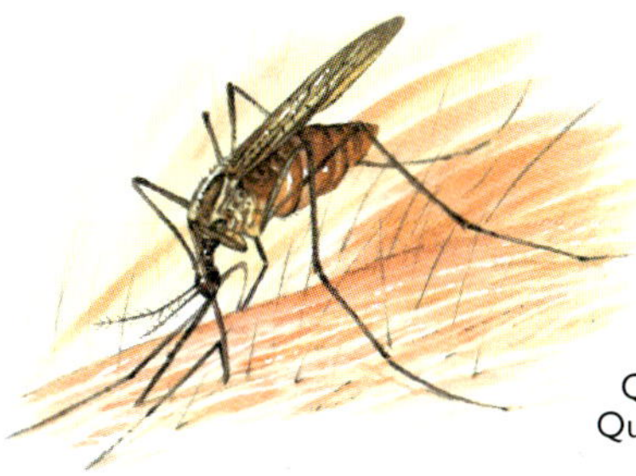

Quiz 101
Question 15

Quiz 103 Level 3

Questions		*Answers*
1	In which war did British troops recapture Port Stanley?	*Falklands War (1982)*
2	Who served as US president before Bill Clinton?	*George Bush*
3	Which organization, that uses the initials RNLI, was founded in 1824?	*Royal National Lifeboat Institution*
4	Which war was fought in Asia from 1950 to 1953?	*Korean War*
5	Who discovered that blood circulates around the body?	*William Harvey*
6	Was the Battle of Midway (1942) fought at sea or on land?	*At sea*
7	What is Louis-Antoine de Bougainville's claim to fame?	*He led first French voyage around the world*
8	Which writer created both Mr Pickwick and Ebenezer Scrooge?	*Charles Dickens*
9	Who was the first woman to be British prime minister?	*Margaret Thatcher*
10	Of which country was Sun Yat-sen president?	*China*
11	What is the name for heaven, according to the Vikings?	*Valhalla*
12	Which continent did Edward Bransfield and Nathaniel Palmer sight in 1820?	*Antarctica*
13	What was the operation called that forced Saddam Hussein out of Kuwait?	*Operation Desert Storm*
14	Who led the Third Crusade in 1189?	*Richard I*
15	What was a Patriot missile designed to shoot down?	*Other missiles*

Quiz 104 Question 11

Quiz 104 Question 14

Quiz 104 Level 3

Questions			Answers
1		What is the first letter in the Greek alphabet?	*Alpha*
2		Who was the Roman god of war?	*Mars*
3		Who was the youngest person ever to be elected US president at the age of 43?	*John F. Kennedy*
4		What region of the world did Hernando de Soto explore in the 1500s?	*The American Southwest*
5		Joseph Lister first used carbolic acid to kill germs during surgery in which year: 1805, 1865 or 1895?	*1865*
6		In which country were soccer's 1998 World Cup finals held?	*France*
7		In which sport were Ayrton Senna and Jackie Stewart world champions?	*Motor racing (Grand Prix)*
8		Which people fought in regiments called impis?	*The Zulus*
9		How did sugar cane and wheat reach America in the 1500s?	*The Spanish brought them*
10		Where is the Khyber Pass, scene of a famous 19th-century massacre?	*Afghanistan-Pakistan border*
11		What form of transport, invented by the Chinese, was a junk?	*A sailing ship*
12		Which actress married Prince Rainier of Monaco before being killed in a car accident in 1982?	*Grace Kelly*
13		In which century did the Russian composer Piotr Tchaikovsky live?	*19th century (1840–1893)*
14		Which type of planes competed for the Schneider Trophy?	*Sea planes*
15		The Romans believed they had to travel across a river to the afterlife. What was the river called?	*River Styx*

Quiz 103
Question 3

Quiz 103
Question 14

Quiz 105 Level 3

	Questions	*Answers*
1	What city was split between the Allies after World War II?	*Berlin*
2	Which country is also known as Hellas?	*Greece*
3	Which two countries fought the Opium War of 1839?	*Britain and China*
4	What was El Dorado?	*A mythical city of gold in South America*
5	Where was the ancient city of Carthage?	*Near modern Tunis, in north Africa*
6	Which king gave up the British throne in 1936?	*Edward VIII (later Duke of Windsor)*
7	Who won the battle of New Orleans in 1815?	*The Americans (they beat the British)*
8	After whom is Frobisher Bay in Canada named?	*The English explorer Martin Frobisher*
9	Which two Middle Eastern countries were at war from 1980 to 1988?	*Iran and Iraq*
10	In which Irish city was James Joyce's novel, *Ulysses*, set?	*Dublin*
11	The sedan chair originated in Italy and arrived in England in 1634. What is it?	*A single enclosed seat carried on poles*
12	On which continent did people look for King Solomon's Mines?	*Africa*
13	What 'first ever' did Matthew Webb achieve in 1875?	*He swam the English Channel*
14	The Black Death reached England in 1348. What was the Black Death?	*An epidemic of bubonic plague*
15	Which festive bird came to European tables from America in the 1500s?	*The turkey*

Quiz 106
Question 6

Quiz 106 Level 3

	Questions	Answers
1	What kind of aircraft, first built in 1939 by Igor Sikorsky, has rotor blades?	*A helicopter*
2	In 1610 Henry Hudson sailed into Hudson Bay: but where did he think he was?	*The Pacific Ocean*
3	Which sport uses racquets and was invented in England in the 1800s?	*Tennis*
4	Which king built a huge palace and church called the Escorial?	*Philip II of Spain*
5	Which continent did Mungo Park explore in the early 1800s?	*Africa*
6	About which French invasion of Russia did Tchaikovsky compose a piece of music?	*Napoleon's invasion in 1812*
7	Where did the US *Pathfinder* spacecraft land in July 1997?	*Mars*
8	Which is the world's biggest glider, first used in 1982?	*The US space shuttle*
9	Which 17th-century English poet continued writing after he became blind?	*John Milton*
10	Which North African city was first visited by Europeans in the 1820s?	*Timbuktu*
11	In which country did the Satsuma Rebellion occur?	*Japan (1877)*
12	Who wrote *The Jungle Book?*	*Rudyard Kipling*
13	In which war was the war poet Wilfred Owen killed?	*World War I (in 1918)*
14	Who made the first solo round-the-world-flight?	*Wiley Post (1933)*
15	When did the US adopt the Star Spangled Banner as the national anthem?	*March 3, 1931*

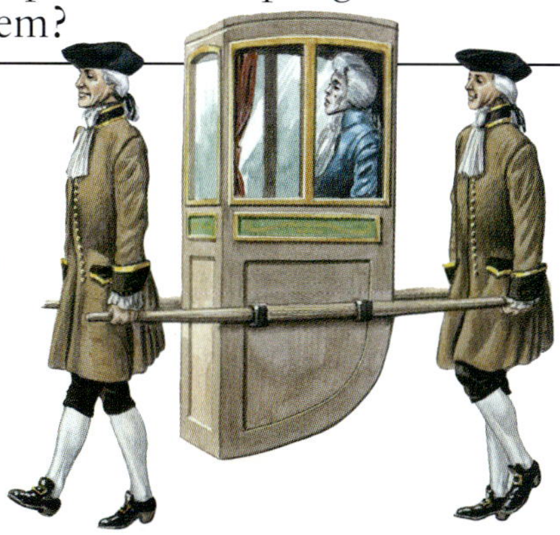

Quiz 105
Question 11

Quiz 107 Level 3

Questions		Answers
1	When did the last Ice Age end: 1 million, 10,000 or 1,000 years ago?	*10,000 years ago*
2	Who fought against Rome in the Punic wars?	*Carthage*
3	What were aqueducts used for in ancient Rome?	*Bringing water*
4	What kind of gun was the Colt 45?	*A revolver*
5	Who is the father of Britain's princes William and Harry?	*Charles, Prince of Wales*
6	Which plane first flew in July 1989?	B-2 Spirit *stealth bomber*
7	In which country does the story of the opera *Madam Butterfly* take place?	*Japan*
8	Who was the most famous European explorer in Africa?	*David Livingstone*
9	In which war did Montgomery and Patton become famous generals?	*World War II (1939-1945)*
10	Who wrote the music for the opera *Porgy and Bess* in 1935?	*George Gershwin*
11	Of which international organization did Kofi Annan became Secretary General in 1997?	*United Nations*
12	Who commanded the army that beat the French at Waterloo in 1815?	*The Duke of Wellington*
13	How old was Alexander the Great when he died: 33, 53 or 63?	*33*
14	In 1863 James Speke discovered the source of the world's longest river, which river?	*The Nile*
15	Which sort of scanning did Ian Donal develop in the 1950s?	*Ultrasound*

Quiz 108 Question 2

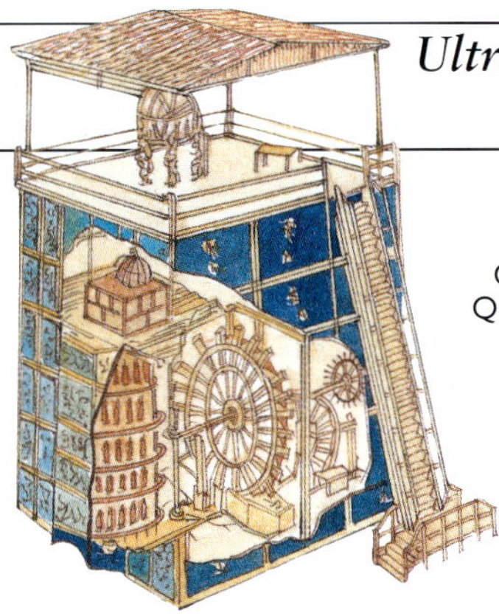

Quiz 108 Question 12

Quiz 108 Level 3

	Questions	Answers
1	Which great Italian city was sacked by the Goths in AD410?	*Rome*
2	The Geiger counter was invented in 1913 to measure what?	*Radioactivity*
3	Which African river did Henry Morton Stanley explore in the 1870s?	*The Congo*
4	Which Australian tennis star was nicknamed 'The Rockhampton Rocket'?	*Rod Laver*
5	Are reptiles' eggs hard-shelled, or leathery?	*Leathery*
6	Were helicopters used in World War I?	*No: they were not used in war until the 1940s*
7	Which arabic sailor featured in *The Arabian Nights*?	*Sinbad*
8	Who was called the father of psychoanalysis?	*Sigmund Freud*
9	How did the explorers Burke and Wills meet their deaths?	*They starved to death in Australia*
10	Was Calamity Jane a real person?	*Yes: her real name was Martha Jane Canary*
11	Which type of sport is Indianapolis famous for?	*'Indy' racing – or motor racing*
12	In 1090, the Chinese built the Cosmic Engine. Did it measure time, rainfall or plant growth?	*Time, it was an early mechanical clock*
13	What nationality was General Pershing?	*American*
14	Which is the biggest selling car of all time?	*The Volkswagen Beetle*
15	Which Norwegian artist painted *The Scream*?	*Edvard Munch*

Quiz 107
Question 8

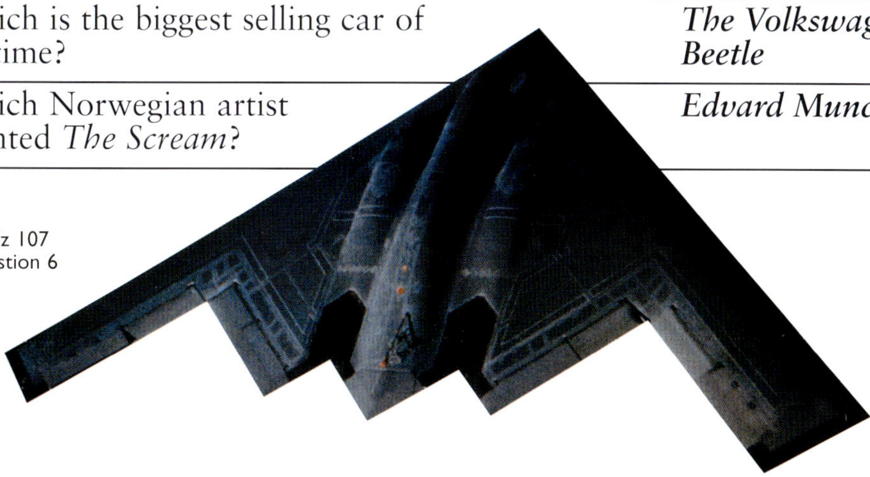

Quiz 107
Question 6

Quiz 109 Level 3

	Questions	*Answers*
1	What was the main Viking weapon, apart from the sword and spear?	*The battle-axe*
2	Of which country was François Mitterand leader?	*France*
3	Which inventor was called 'The Wizard of Menlo Park'?	*Edison (Menlo Park was the site of his laboratory)*
4	Where did soldiers wear armour called greaves?	*On their shins*
5	What was the nickname for Britain's Home Guard during World War II?	*Dad's Army*
6	The world's first civilization was 'the land between two rivers'. What do we call it?	*Mesopotamia*
7	Avicenna was a famous Persian doctor, writer or soldier?	*Doctor*
8	What name was given to a Norse warrior wearing bearskins who went crazy in battle?	*A berserker*
9	The first Chinese emperor was buried with an army of life-size soldiers. What were they made of?	*Terracotta*
10	What kind of aircraft was the World War II Catalina?	*A flying boat*
11	What was Edison's kinetoscope?	*A peephole machine, for watching short films*
12	When was the first armoured car built?	*1904*
13	In which sport did Carl Lewis become a star?	*Track and field athletics*
14	On which planet did the *Venera 7* space probe land in 1970?	*Venus*
15	Which Welsh poet wrote *Under Milk Wood*?	*Dylan Thomas*

Quiz 110 Question 7

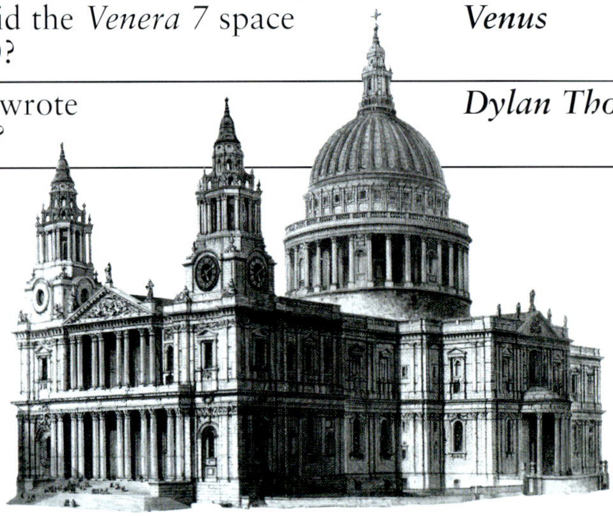

Quiz 110 Question 2

Quiz 110 Level 3

	Questions	Answers
1	What kind of lamp did Joseph Swan invent?	*The electric lamp*
2	Which great cathedral was completed in 1717?	*St Paul's Cathedral*
3	Who was US president for most of World War II?	*Franklin D. Roosevelt*
4	What kind of fish was the star of the *Jaws* films?	*A great white shark*
5	What weapon was fixed to the bow of an ancient Egyptian warship?	*A ram for sinking enemy ships*
6	What were the main divisions of the Roman army called?	*Legions*
7	Which people were probably the first to 'discover' America?	*The Vikings*
8	The powerful ancient 'composite' bow was made of wood, animal sinew and what?	*Horn*
9	What garment did a Roman man drape over his tunic?	*A toga*
10	Could Abraham Lincoln have met George Washington?	*No: Washington died before Lincoln was born*
11	Who wrote horror tales such as *The Fall of the House of Usher?*	*Edgar Allan Poe*
12	Which modern country made up most of Gaul in Roman times?	*France*
13	What nationality was the physicist Hans Christian Oersted (1777-1851)?	*Danish*
14	Which hunting weapon used by Australian aboriginals was also used by ancient Egyptians?	*The boomerang*
15	Did the coffee plant originally grow wild in Africa or South America?	*Africa*

Quiz 109
Question 10

Quiz 109
Question 14

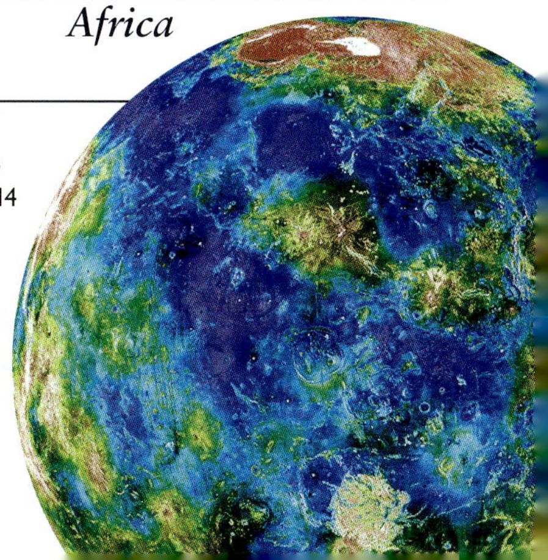

Quiz 111 Level 3

	Questions	Answers
1	In which war did the city of Saigon fall?	*The Vietnam War*
2	Of which country was Golda Meir a famous leader?	*Israel*
3	Of what was Sir George Cayley (1753-1857) a pioneer?	*Flight (he built experimental gliders)*
4	Who or what were fighter aces?	*Pilots who shot down many enemy planes*
5	Was the jitterbug a dance or a disease?	*A dance popular in the 1940s*
6	Who built an early steamship called the *Clermont*?	*Robert Fulton*
7	What did Dick Rutan and Jeanna Yeager do in nine days in 1986?	*Flew round the world without refuelling*
8	"Once more into the breach dear friends" were words attributed to King Henry V by whom?	*William Shakespeare*
9	Who wrote *Robinson Crusoe?*	*Daniel Defoe*
10	The Roman gladiator called a *retiarius* fought with a net and which other weapon?	*A trident*
11	When did people first wear nylon clothing: 1930s, 1950s, or 1970s?	*1930s*
12	Who wiped out three Roman legions in the Teutoburger forest in AD9?	*German tribes*
13	Who was married to the Empress Josephine?	*Napoleon Bonaparte*
14	In which books does a wizard called Gandalf appear?	The Hobbit *and* The Lord of the Rings
15	Which Queen Mary was executed in 1587?	*Mary Queen of Scots*

Quiz 112
Question 2

Quiz 112
Question 10

Quiz 112 Level 3

	Questions	Answers
1	Where does the curious crawling parrot called the kakapo live?	*New Zealand*
2	Who was the 19th-century founder of Communism?	*Karl Marx*
3	Which of Shakespeare's plays is about a black soldier?	Othello
4	Which are the biggest and most powerful warships today?	*Aircraft carriers*
5	Captain Cook fed his crew on 'sour krout': what was it?	*Cabbage pickled in vinegar*
6	Did eating too many potatoes make King Henry VIII so fat?	*No. He died before they reached England*
7	Which medical instrument for listening to the sounds of the chest was invented in 1819?	*The stethoscope*
8	Against whom was Robert the Bruce fighting when he was inspired to try again by a spider?	*King Edward II of England*
9	What was the name of the short, stabbing sword used by the Roman soldiers?	*Gladius*
10	What was special about the dinosaur called stegosaurus?	*It had jagged plates on its back*
11	Renoir, Rembrandt and Reynolds were all . . . what?	*Painters*
12	Why did sailing warships have copper bottoms?	*To stop seaworms boring holes in the wood*
13	John Hunter was an important figure in which field of medicine?	*Surgery*
14	What was the Crystal Palace?	*A huge glass and steel building (London 1851)*
15	Which country developed the first atomic bomb?	*USA*

Quiz 111 Question 8

Quiz 111 Question 15

Quiz 111 Question 13

Quiz 113 Level 3

Questions		Answers
1	What did Native Americans do with pemmican?	*They ate it (it was dried meat)*
2	Of which country were Brian Mulroney and Pierre Trudeau prime ministers?	*Canada*
3	Why did Joseph Lister use carbolic acid in operating rooms?	*To kill germs and prevent infection*
4	Stephen Crane wrote *The Red Badge of Courage:* about which war?	*The American Civil War*
5	How many players from West Ham were in the England team that won the World Cup in 1966?	*Three*
6	Which one of these was invented in the 18th century: steam vehicle, radio, microscope?	*Steam vehicle*
7	Who was it that was restored in the 'Restoration' in England in 1660?	*Charles II (to the throne of England)*
8	What did sailors use hammocks for?	*They slept in them*
9	A tower in Paris is named after him; he also designed the skeleton for the Statue of Liberty. What was his name?	*Alexandre Eiffel*
10	Which unit of power, invented by James Watt, measures the output of an engine?	*Horsepower*
11	Who led a peasants' rebellion in England in 1381?	*Wat Tyler*
12	In what year was the first 'test-tube' baby born?	*1978*
13	Why was there fighting in India in 1857?	*It was the year of the Indian Mutiny*
14	Which was the only dinosaur to have three horns?	*Triceratops*
15	Which composer wrote the *Young Person's Guide to the Orchestra?*	*Benjamin Britten*

Quiz 114
Question 6

Quiz 114
Question 15

Quiz 114 Level 3

	Questions	Answers
1	Which pop stars made a film called *A Hard Day's Night?*	*The Beatles*
2	Where did Peary and Henson go in 1909?	*Portugal*
3	Who was Geronimo?	*An Apache Indian Chief*
4	With what invention is Robert Oppenheimer (1904-1967) associated?	*The atomic bomb*
5	Which Christian saint was sent by the Pope to convert the English in AD597?	*Augustine*
6	Which was the most important British fighter plane to be used in the Battle of Britain?	*The Hurricane*
7	Of which country is David the patron saint?	*Wales*
8	How many labours did Hercules have to perform?	*Twelve*
9	How many shots could a musket fire before being reloaded?	*One*
10	In the Bible, who was thrown into a lion's den for defying King Nebuchadnezzar?	*Daniel*
11	Of what country was Henry the Navigator a prince (in the 1400s)?	*Portugal*
12	With which rock group did Mick Jagger find fame?	*The Rolling Stones*
13	Who composed the *William Tell Overture?*	*Rossini*
14	What is the ancient Japanese art of bonsai?	*Growing miniature trees*
15	Of which country was Mussolini leader from 1922 to 1943?	*Italy*

Quiz 113
Question 7

Quiz 113
Question 14

Quiz 115 Level 4

	Questions	Answers
1	Which was the first make of car to be produced on an assembly line?	*The Ford Model T*
2	Which serving British prime minister survived an assassination attempt?	*Margaret Thatcher*
3	Which jeweller became famous for the fabulous Easter eggs he made for the Russian royal family?	*Carl Fabergé*
4	Which old English coin was nicknamed a 'tanner'?	*Six old pence*
5	In which country did the Maya people build pyramids?	*Mexico*
6	What was boxer Muhammad Ali's original name?	*Cassius Clay*
7	On which island is Osborne House, home of Queen Victoria?	*Isle of Wight*
8	Which Asian country was led by dictator Pol Pot?	*Cambodia*
9	Who is the arch enemy of Sherlock Holmes?	*Professor Moriarty*
10	Early cars had windscreens made of glass: true or false?	*True*
11	Which Quaker family founded a chocolate factory in York?	*Rowntree*
12	Which 18th-century Austrian composer had the Christian names, Wolfgang Amadeus?	*Mozart*
13	What was film star Herbie?	*A VW Beetle car*
14	What simple weapon did Samson use, according to the Bible, to defeat the Philistines?	*An ass's jawbone*
15	What kind of bomber was a World War II Stuka?	*Dive-bomber*

Quiz 116
Question 15

Quiz 116
Question 1

Quiz 116 Level 4

Questions		*Answers*
1	Who danced the 'dance of the seven veils'?	*Salome*
2	What sort of place was 'Bedlam' in 18th-century London?	*A lunatic asylum*
3	In which country was the high speed TGV train introduced in 1967?	*France*
4	What instrument did jazz legend Louis Armstrong play?	*Trumpet*
5	What style were the piano compositions of Scott Joplin – ragtime, classical or jazz?	*Ragtime*
6	What Native American boat was used by early explorers on narrow rivers?	*The canoe*
7	Which English poet created *The Jumblies* and *The Dong with the Luminous Nose*?	*Edward Lear*
8	In which battle was King Harold killed?	*Hastings*
9	Which river was Jesus baptized in?	*The Jordan*
10	In which war was the Battle of Verdun?	*World War I*
11	Where would a medieval knight have worn a cuirass?	*On his chest and back*
12	In the Bible, which of Jacob's sons had a coat of many colours?	*Joseph*
13	In the Bible, who were the two sons of Adam and Eve?	*Cain and Abel*
14	Manet and Monet were both Impressionist painters: true or false?	*True*
15	For what invention are the Montgolfier brothers remembered?	*The first successful hot-air balloon*

Quiz 115
Question 12

Quiz 115
Question 3

Quiz 115
Question 1

Quiz 117 Level 4

#	Questions	*Answers*
1	Gladys Knight sang the theme song for which Bond film?	Licence to Kill
2	Which Jewish girl kept a diary whilst hidden in Amsterdam in 1942?	*Anne Frank*
3	On which continent mainland did Columbus land for the first time in 1498?	*South America*
4	Who was the second man to walk on the Moon?	*Edwin 'Buzz' Aldrin*
5	What is the most common name for an English monarch?	*Henry (8 times)*
6	What was the horse-powered postal service of the 'Wild West'?	*The Pony Express*
7	In what decade was the first Star Wars film released?	*The 1970s*
8	Who was the greatest knight of King Arthur's Round Table?	*Sir Lancelot*
9	Where would an armoured knight have worn greaves?	*On his shins*
10	Which modern household pet was sacred in Ancient Egypt?	*The cat*
11	Which World War II fighter aircraft was made mainly of wood?	*The Mosquito*
12	What vital modern medicine was discovered by Alexander Fleming in 1928?	*Penicillin*
13	Whose Gospel comes first in the New Testament of the Bible?	*Matthew*
14	Which novelist invented the characters of Samuel Pickwick, Bill Sykes and Little Nell?	*Charles Dickens*
15	Who invented the aqualung in 1943?	*Jacques Cousteau*

Quiz 118
Question 2

Quiz 118
Question 6

Quiz 118 Level 4

Questions		*Answers*
1	Who devised a method of map projection which is named after him?	*Mercator*
2	What did Rip Van Winkle do for twenty years, in Washington Irving's tale?	*Slept*
3	Which railway line, built between 1891 and 1905, is the world's longest?	*The Trans-Siberian railway*
4	Which characters in the Bible had no uncles or aunts and only one set of grandparents?	*Cain and Abel*
5	What did Charles Richter invent a scale to measure the strength of?	*Earthquakes*
6	Which part of Cyrano de Bergerac was unusually large?	*His nose*
7	Which is the second book in the Bible?	*Exodus*
8	Valentina Tereshkova was the first woman to do what in 1963?	*Travel in space*
9	What famous landmark was built to celebrate the Paris Exhibition of 1889?	*The Eiffel Tower*
10	In which war did the Royalists fight the Parliamentarians?	*English Civil War*
11	Which Egyptian queen was loved by both Julius Caesar and Mark Antony?	*Cleopatra*
12	Which fictional detective was created by Arthur Conan Doyle?	*Sherlock Holmes*
13	Which space telescope is named after a US astronomer?	*Hubble*
14	What name was given to Japanese suicide pilots of World War II?	*Kamikaze*
15	Arnold Schwarzenegger was born in Canada: true or false?	*False*

Quiz 117
Question 14

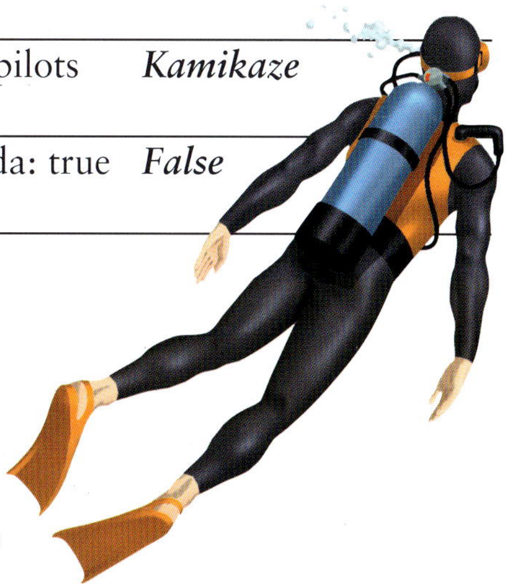

Quiz 117
Question 15

Quiz 119 Level 4

	Questions	Answers
1	Which instrument is associated with Yehudi Menuhin?	*The violin*
2	What were the Christian names of Laurel and Hardy?	*Stanley and Oliver*
3	What caused the *Titanic* to sink?	*It hit an iceberg*
4	America was the New World: where was the Old World?	*Europe and Asia*
5	Who fought to unify Italy with an army of 1,000 'Redshirts'?	*Giuseppe Garibaldi*
6	What was the Eiffel Tower made of?	*Metal*
7	Who wrote about a hedgehog called Mrs Tiggywinkle?	*Beatrix Potter*
8	What nationality was Alexander Graham Bell, inventor of the telephone?	*Scottish*
9	Who led the Argonauts on their search for the Golden Fleece?	*Jason*
10	Which war was fought between the Union and the Confederacy?	*American Civil War*
11	What kind of weapon was Big Bertha?	*A giant long-range cannon*
12	Which highwayman rode Black Bess?	*Dick Turpin*
13	Which Shakespeare play was the basis for the musical *West Side Story*?	Romeo and Juliet
14	Was a Douglas Dakota a tank, an aircraft or a landing vessel?	*An aircraft*
15	What does the Bayeux Tapestry show?	*The Norman invasion of England*

Quiz 120
Question 11

Quiz 120
Question 10

Quiz 120 Level 4

Questions		Answers
1	Which of Jesus's disciples was described as 'Doubting'?	*Thomas*
2	What does E stand for in Einstein's famous equation $E=mc^2$?	*Energy*
3	Who painted the ceiling of the Sistine Chapel in Rome?	*Michelangelo*
4	What was used to execute people during the French Revolution's 'Reign of Terror'?	*The guillotine*
5	By what name was Zimbabwe previously known?	*Rhodesia*
6	What type of shop first opened in Britain in 1948?	*A supermarket*
7	Which was the first faster-than-sound aircraft to take commercial passengers?	*Concorde*
8	Which murderer terrorized part of London in 1888?	*Jack the Ripper*
9	Which war began after the assassination of Archduke Ferdinand in Sarajevo?	*World War 1*
10	In World War II, what was a Messerschmitt ME-110?	*A German bomber*
11	What was the name of the highly-trained killers of feudal Japan?	*Ninjas*
12	Who wrote *The Brandenburg Concertos*?	*J.S. Bach*
13	What is the last book in the Bible?	*Revelation*
14	What kind of aircraft was a Short Sunderland?	*A seaplane*
15	What is carved on Mount Rushmore in the USA?	*Heads of four presidents*

Quiz 119 Question 7

Quiz 119 Question 5

Quiz 121 Level 4

Questions / *Answers*

	Questions	Answers
1	Who wrote *Journey to the Centre of the Earth*?	*Jules Verne*
2	In which range of mountains was the Abominable Snowman sighted?	*The Himalayas*
3	Who did Peeping Tom peep at in about 1040?	*Lady Godiva*
4	What kind of animal was the first to go into space?	*A dog*
5	Who wrote the poem "If…"?	*Rudyard Kipling*
6	Which cricketer holds the records for highest Test score (375) and highest first-class score (501)?	*Brian Lara*
7	Which songbird was discovered on the Canary Islands in the 15th century?	*The canary*
8	What did medieval alchemists hope to do with ordinary metals?	*Turn them into gold*
9	Which weapon was invented in Bayonne in about 1590?	*The bayonet*
10	Which footballer claimed that his 1986 World Cup goal was helped by the hand of God?	*Diego Maradona*
11	Who wrote the song 'Roll Over Beethoven'?	*Chuck Berry*
12	Where was the first known dam built – in ancient China, Greece or Egypt?	*Egypt*
13	Who was the first Tudor monarch of Britain?	*Henry VII*
14	How many of Henry VIII's wives were beheaded?	*Two*
15	Name one of the Axis powers of World War II.	*Germany, Italy, Japan*

Quiz 122
Question 9

Quiz 122
Question 8

Quiz 122 Level 4

	Questions	Answers
1	What was the 'Charleston'?	*A dance*
2	Which rock star burned his guitar on stage in 1967?	*Jimi Hendrix*
3	Who was the wife of King Arthur?	*Guinevere*
4	Who walked to the South Pole and flew to the North Pole?	*Amundsen*
5	What was the name of the Russian space station?	Mir
6	Who produced multiple screen prints of Marilyn Monroe's face?	*Andy Warhol*
7	Who was the Roman goddess of hunting?	*Diana*
8	Who was the Greek god of the sea?	*Neptune*
9	Which side used a Trojan Horse to enter the city of Troy?	*The Greeks*
10	Who worked out the Theory of Relativity?	*Einstein*
11	What was the huge glass building erected in London for the Great Exhibition in 1851?	*The Crystal Palace*
12	Who was shot by John Wilkes Booth in 1865?	*Abraham Lincoln*
13	In which US city was the first skyscraper built in 1885?	*Chicago*
14	Which film told the story of the 'bouncing bombs' of World War II?	The Dambusters
15	In which war did the Battle of Balaclava take place in 1854?	*The Crimean War*

Quiz 121 Question 4

Quiz 121 Question 7

Quiz 121 Question 9

Quiz 123 Level 4

	Questions	Answers
1	Who discovered the law of gravity?	*Isaac Newton*
2	Who wrote the novel *War and Peace*?	*Leo Tolstoy*
3	How did Julius Caesar die?	*He was stabbed*
4	Who wrote *The War of the Worlds*?	*H.G.Wells*
5	What did test pilot Chuck Yeager break in 1947?	*The sound barrier*
6	In which city would you find the Rialto bridge?	*Venice*
7	What kind of weapon was an arquebus?	*An early form of musket (firearm)*
8	What does the Statue of Liberty hold in her right hand?	*A torch*
9	Who had a price ticket in his hat in a Lewis Carroll story?	*The Mad Hatter*
10	What nationality is Pope John Paul II?	*Polish*
11	What name did Malcolm and Donald Campbell give their various high-speed vehicles?	Bluebird
12	What kind of firearm was patented by Samuel Colt in 1835?	*The revolver*
13	What country did Cleopatra rule?	*Ancient Egypt*
14	What name was given to the US programme to land on the Moon?	Apollo
15	In which decade was the Korean war fought?	*The 1950s*

Quiz124
Question 12

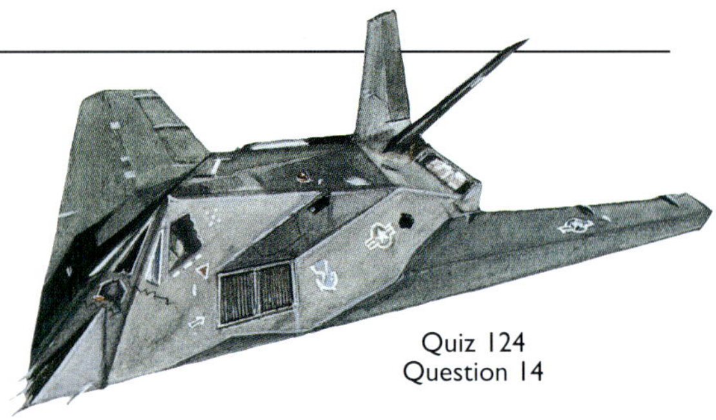

Quiz 124
Question 14

Quiz 124 Level 4

	Questions	Answers
1	What, in the USA, is known as 'Old Glory'?	*The national flag*
2	What kind of firearm was developed by Oliver Winchester in 1866?	*The repeating rifle*
3	Which married couple won the Nobel Prize for Science in 1903?	*Marie and Pierre Curie*
4	Who wrote *Under Milk Wood*?	*Dylan Thomas*
5	When was the Berlin Wall built: 1941, 1961 or 1981?	*1961*
6	What fills the bottle of a Molotov cocktail?	*Petrol*
7	What nationality was Pablo Picasso?	*Spanish*
8	How many states were there in the original United States of America?	*13*
9	How often (to within five years) does Halley's Comet fly near the earth?	*Every 75 years*
10	When was the first submarine built: 1624, 1824 or 1924?	*1624*
11	What material, beginning with P, did the Ancient Egyptians write on?	*Papyrus*
12	What famous World War II fighter plane was developed from a seaplane?	*The Spitfire*
13	Which notorious Australian robber was hanged at Melbourne in 1880?	*Ned Kelly*
14	Why is the US 'Stealth' fighter so called?	*Because it is difficult to detect on radar*
15	What long poem did Oscar Wilde write in prison?	The Ballad of Reading Gaol

Quiz 123
Question 1

Quiz 123
Question 11

Quiz 123
Question 9

Quiz 125 Level 4

	Questions	Answers
1	Who were the Light Brigade charging against?	*The Russians*
2	What did John McAdam become famous for?	*Road-making*
3	Who dreamed up *The Invisible Man*?	*H.G.Wells*
4	What was invented by Isaac Singer in 1851?	*The sewing machine*
5	What is the five-sided office of the US Defense Department called?	*The Pentagon*
6	In which band did Bill Wyman play for over twenty years?	*The Rolling Stones*
7	Bakelite was an early form of what modern material?	*Plastic*
8	Who were the Texans fighting at the Alamo?	*The Mexicans*
9	Who was the king of France when the Revolution began: Louis XIV or Louis XVI?	*Louis XVI*
10	What did William Tell use to shoot an apple from his son's head?	*A crossbow*
11	Which navy did the battle cruiser *Bismarck* belong to?	*German*
12	Who was the USA's tallest-ever president?	*Abraham Lincoln*
13	Who wrote the *1812 Overture*?	*Tchaikovsky*
14	What huge beasts were used by the Carthaginians at the Battle of Zama in 202BC?	*Elephants*
15	Who founded the Scout movement?	*Robert Baden-Powell*

Quiz 126
Question 9

Quiz 126
Question 13

Quiz 126 Level 4

Questions / *Answers*

	Questions	Answers
1	What was the only novel written by Emily Brontë?	**Wuthering Heights**
2	From which country does opera singer Kiri Te Kanawa come?	***New Zealand***
3	How many pre-decimal pennies were there in a shilling?	***12***
4	Which fictional pirate had a parrot called Captain Flint?	***Long John Silver***
5	Which scientist's name is given to the heat treatment of milk?	***Louis Pasteur (pasteurization)***
6	In the Roman army, which unit was bigger: a legion or a cohort?	***Legion***
7	Who, in the Bible, was the brother of Esau?	***Jacob***
8	Which planet was the last to be discovered?	***Pluto***
9	Which leader won the Battle of Austerlitz in 1805?	***Napoleon***
10	Benito Mussolini ruled which European country in the 20th century?	***Italy***
11	What kind of weapon is a bazooka?	***A hand-held rocket launcher***
12	Who was Britain's youngest ever prime minister?	***William Pitt the Younger***
13	Whose tomb did Howard Carter find in 1922?	***Tutankhamun***
14	Which Russian scientist trained hungry dogs to salivate at the sound of a bell?	***Ivan Pavlov***
15	Who are the Nepalese soldiers who have served with the British Army since World War I?	***The Gurkhas***

Quiz 125
Question 4

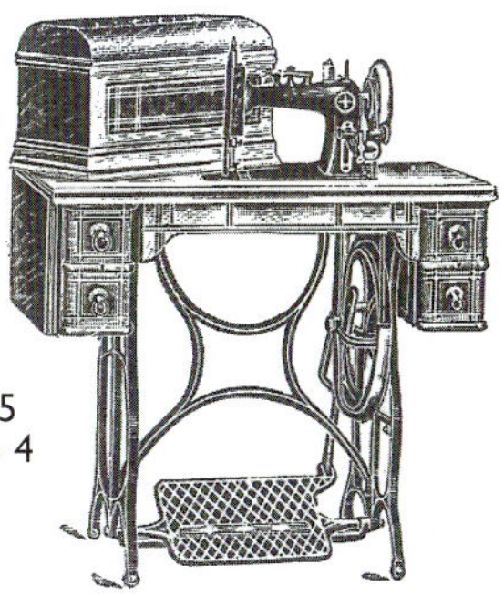

Quiz 125
Question 13

Quiz 127 Level 4

	Questions	Answers
1	Of which country was Ferdinand Marcos dictator?	*The Philippines*
2	Who built the first successful helicopter?	*Igor Sikorsky*
3	What did Walter Raleigh go to search for in South America in 1595 and 1617?	*El Dorado*
4	How many Gospels are there in the New Testament of the Bible?	*Four*
5	Which army was founded by William and Catherine Booth?	*The Salvation Army*
6	Which Israeli prime minister was assassinated in 1995?	*Yitzhak Rabin*
7	Which South American country once had Juan Perón as president?	*Argentina*
8	Who was wrecked on the shore of Lilliput island?	*Gulliver in Swift's* Gulliver's Travels
9	What kind of engines were pioneered by Robert Goddard and Wernher von Braun?	*Rocket engines*
10	Who wrote the poem 'Stopping by Woods on a Snowy Evening'?	*Robert Frost*
11	Chinese sailors threw stones or bags of gravel overboard as an early form of what?	*Anchor*
12	Who ruled England first: Mary I or Elizabeth I?	*Mary I*
13	Name three types of power that trains use.	*Steam, diesel, electricity*
14	Who was the first European to sail around Cape Horn?	*Francis Drake*
15	Was Le Corbusier a painter, an architect or a film director?	*Architect*

Quiz 128
Question 7

Quiz 128
Question 8

Quiz 128 Level 4

Questions		*Answers*
1	Between which two cities did the first regular passenger flights start in 1919?	*Paris and London*
2	Who starred in the films *The Gold Rush* and *Modern Times*?	*Charlie Chaplin*
3	Which two elements in the air were first named by Lavoisier in 1777?	*Oxygen and nitrogen*
4	Which king led the English at the Battle of Agincourt?	*Henry V*
5	In which country was Europe's first motorway built?	*Germany*
6	Which conqueror led his army from Greece to western India?	*Alexander the Great*
7	In World War II, what were Shermans and Panzers?	*Tanks*
8	Which cricketer had the Christian names William Gilbert?	*W.G. Grace*
9	Who, in Greek mythology, had snakes instead of hair?	*Medusa*
10	Which ocean was Balboa the first European to see in 1513?	*Pacific*
11	What kind of products did Thomas Sheraton design and make?	*Furniture*
12	Which Chinese leader wrote *The Little Red Book*?	*Mao tse-Tung*
13	Which Australian state is named after the man who discovered it?	*Tasmania*
14	Which British king gave his name to a kind of potato?	*King Edward (VII)*
15	Which French painter of the 19th century went to live in the South Seas?	*Paul Gauguin*

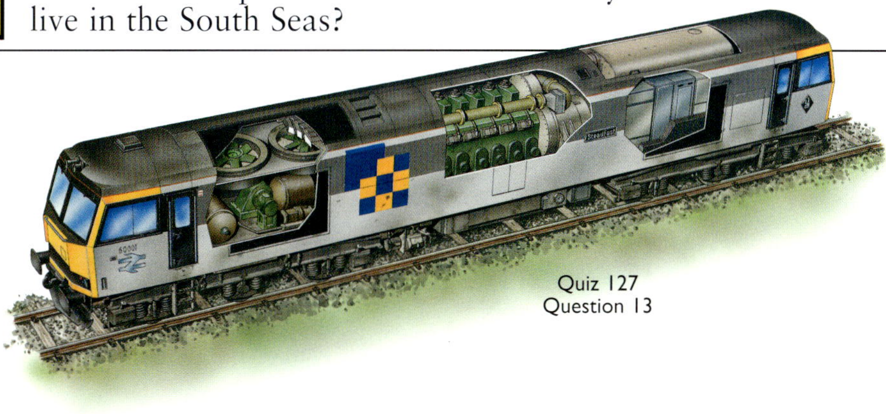

Quiz 127
Question 13

Quiz 129 Level 4

	Questions	Answers
1	Which country was ruled by Ayatolla Khomeini until 1989?	*Iran*
2	Which Mediterranean island was awarded the George Cross for bravery in 1942?	*Malta*
3	What is the name of the motorized sledge driven on snowy surfaces?	*Skidoo*
4	Which African desert was René Caillié the first European to cross in 1828?	*The Sahara*
5	Which country was ruled by Achmed Sukarno until 1967?	*Indonesia*
6	What did the Egyptian god of the dead Anubis look like?	*A man with a jackal's head*
7	Which Australian city did the singer Dame Nellie Melba come from?	*Melbourne*
8	From where did Galileo drop a lead ball and a wooden ball as an experiment?	*The Leaning Tower of Pisa*
9	Who was the only undefeated world heavyweight boxing champion?	*Rocky Marciano*
10	Which continent is associated with explorer Ernest Shackleton?	*Antarctica*
11	Which Asian colony ceased to be British in 1997?	*Hong Kong*
12	Who wrote *The Water Babies*?	*Charles Kingsley*
13	What nationality was Mother Theresa?	*Albanian*
14	Where did Noah's Ark come to rest after the flood?	*Mount Ararat*
15	Who was the first person to fly over the North and South Poles?	*Richard E. Byrd*

Quiz 130
Question 3

Quiz 130
Question 2

Quiz 130 Level 4

	Questions	Answers
1	In which religion is the *Talmud* a sacred text?	*Judaism*
2	What kind of fish attracted 16th-century fishermen to the east coast of North America?	*The cod*
3	Which British commander drove the French from Quebec in 1759?	*James Wolfe*
4	What does an army march on, according to Napoleon?	*Its stomach*
5	Who composed the symphonic poem *Finlandia*?	*Jean Sibelius*
6	Which US president was known as 'Tricky Dicky'?	*Richard Nixon*
7	What make was the first completely waterproof watch (1926)?	*Rolex*
8	Who was elected US president four times?	*Franklin D. Roosevelt*
9	In which year was the Suez Crisis?	*1956*
10	What kind of high-intensity light beam was proposed by Einstein in 1917?	*The laser*
11	Which continent was explored by Frenchman Jacques Cartier in the 1530s?	*North America*
12	Which Hungarian composer was said to be the greatest pianist of the 19th century?	*Franz Liszt*
13	Who were forbidden from watching the Olympic Games in Ancient Greece?	*Women*
14	Which country was led by Kemal Atattürk?	*Turkey*
15	Which modern country was once called Siam?	*Thailand*

Quiz 129
Question 6

Quiz 129
Question 3

Quiz 131 Level 4

Questions / *Answers*

	Question	Answer
1	Which ruler was known as 'The Little Corporal'?	*Napoleon*
2	Which queen became Empress of India in 1876?	*Victoria*
3	What was the city of New York originally called by Dutch settlers?	*New Amsterdam*
4	What very common metal was first extracted from bauxite in 1822?	*Aluminium*
5	Which Greek thinker was condemned to die by drinking poison?	*Socrates*
6	Where did the space probe *Venera 7* land in 1970?	*On Venus*
7	What is the setting for Verdi's opera *Aida*?	*Ancient Egypt*
8	What did Jesus's twelve disciples become known as after his death?	*The Apostles*
9	Who was the longest-serving Australian prime minister?	*Robert Menzies*
10	What is the only part left standing of the ancient Temple of Jerusalem?	*The Western (Wailing) Wall*
11	Which range of mountains was crossed by Lewis and Clark in 1805?	*The Rockies*
12	Which great city was captured by the Turks in 1453?	*Constantinople (Istanbul)*
13	In which year did Adolf Hitler die?	*1945*
14	Which islands off Ecuador inspired Charles Darwin's theory of evolution?	*The Galapagos*
15	How many voyages did Columbus make across the Atlantic?	*Four*

Quiz 132 Question 3

Quiz 132 Question 8

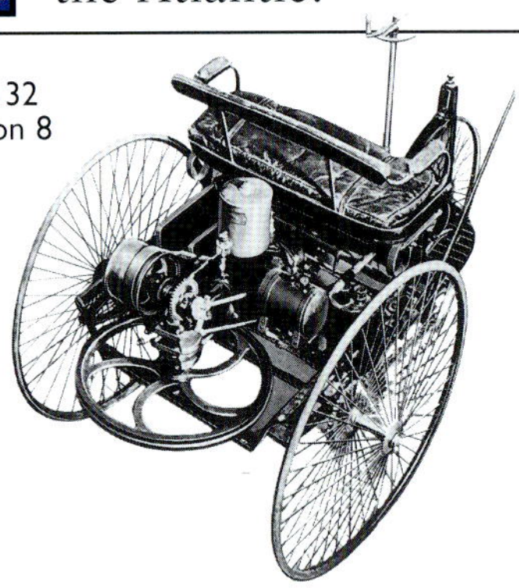

Quiz 132 Question 2

Quiz 132 Level 4

	Questions	Answers
1	In which country was Adolf Hitler born?	*Austria*
2	Which famous car was designed by Alec Issigonis in 1959: the Beetle, the 2CV or the Mini?	*The Mini*
3	Who wrote the original novel of *Les Miserables*?	*Victor Hugo*
4	Winston Churchill was half American: true or false?	*True*
5	What nationality was Abel Tasman, discoverer of New Zealand?	*Dutch*
6	Who was Queen Elizabeth II's father?	*George VI*
7	Which of the Marx Brothers wore a painted false moustache?	*Groucho*
8	The Mercedes Benz car was named after the daughter of an investor: true or false?	*True*
9	What was David Livingstone's job?	*Missionary*
10	In which country was the first national park set up in 1872?	*USA (Yellowstone)*
11	How did African explorer H.M. Stanley earn his living?	*He was a journalist*
12	Horror film actor Boris Karloff was English: true or false?	*True*
13	Which religious sect founded Salt Lake City in the USA?	*The Mormons*
14	Which Norman king of England began the building of the Tower of London?	*William I*
15	In which city is the Kaaba, the holy Muslim building?	*Mecca*

Quiz 133 Question 2

Quiz 133 Question 6

Quiz 133 Level 4

Questions		Answers
1	Which English tax caused riots in 1381 and 1990?	*The Poll Tax*
2	Where did a *Viking* land in 1976?	*Mars*
3	Of which African country was Jomo Kenyatta the first president?	*Kenya*
4	In which country was the Easter Rising of 1916?	*Ireland*
5	What was the spacecraft that made the first Moon landing?	Apollo 11
6	In which city was the first set of traffic lights set up in 1868?	*London*
7	In which war was the Battle of the Bulge?	*World War II*
8	Which US president was known as 'Ike'?	*Dwight Eisenhower*
9	In which harbour did Francis Drake singe the king of Spain's beard?	*Cadiz*
10	What natural wonder is named after aviator James Angel?	*The Angel Falls*
11	In which year was the Battle of Britain?	*1940*
12	In which country would you find the medieval Alhambra palace?	*Spain*
13	Which country funded Columbus's Atlantic voyage: Spain or Portugal?	*Spain*
14	A velocipede was an early name for what form of transport?	*Bicycle*
15	Who became president of France first in 1945 and last in 1968?	*Charles de Gaulle*

Quiz 134 Question 14

Quiz 134 Question 2

Quiz 134 Question 4

Quiz 134 Level 4

	Questions	Answers
1	Who won a record seven gold medals at the 1972 Olympics?	*Mark Spitz*
2	Which English poet died in 1824 helping Greece in her revolt against the Turks?	*Lord Byron*
3	Which European country was ruled by Tito from 1945 to 1980?	*Yugoslavia*
4	What, in ancient Greece, was an amphora?	*A big two-handled vase*
5	What shipboard disease did Captain Cook prevent by taking fresh food and fruit juice?	*Scurvy*
6	Who captained HMS *Victory* at the Battle of Trafalgar?	*Captain Hardy*
7	What was the popular term for the dividing line between the West and the Communist bloc?	*The Iron Curtain*
8	What did Italian dictator Mussolini's title 'Il Duce' mean?	*The Leader*
9	Which Italian city was once ruled by a doge?	*Venice*
10	What was *Early Bird*?	*The first commercial satellite (1965)*
11	What did early sailors call the islands where cinnamon, cloves and nutmegs were grown?	*The Spice Islands*
12	Which holy man became a favourite of the Tsar's family just before the Russian Revolution?	*Rasputin*
13	In which US town did the 'Gunfight at the OK Corral' take place?	*Tombstone, Arizona*
14	Who wrote the horror story *The Pit and the Pendulum*?	*Edgar Allan Poe*
15	Which country was known to explorers as 'The Roof of the World'?	*Tibet*

Quiz 133
Question 10

Quiz 133
Question 5

Quiz 135 Level 4

	Questions	Answers
1	In which country did the poets Keats and Shelley die?	*Italy*
2	How many buffalo did Buffalo Bill slaughter: 40, 400 or 4,000?	*4,000*
3	What sign of the Abominable Snowman has been photographed?	*Footprint*
4	Who reached the Bahamas and thought he had reached India?	*Columbus*
5	How long did an early musket take to reload: 10 seconds, one minute or two minutes?	*Two minutes*
6	What kind of public transport was introduced to London by George Shillibeer in 1829?	*The bus service*
7	Which native peoples call Creation 'The Dream Time'?	*Australian Aboriginals*
8	Which famous American playwright married Marilyn Monroe?	*Arthur Miller*
9	How many ships were there in the Spanish Armada: 30, 130 or 530?	*130*
10	Who was the husband of Queen Victoria?	*Prince Albert*
11	Who owned the famous Wild West Show?	*Buffalo Bill Cody*
12	Who first sailed around Africa to India?	*Vasco da Gama*
13	Of which country was Augusto Pinochet once dictator?	*Chile*
14	Where was Archbishop Thomas Becket murdered in 1170?	*Canterbury Cathedral*
15	Where is China's Forbidden City?	*Beijing*

Quiz 136
Question 15

Quiz 136
Question 13

Quiz 136 Level 4

Questions		*Answers*
1	Who wrote the opera *Carmen*?	*Bizet*
2	Of which ancient country was Akhenaten a ruler?	*Egypt*
3	Which conflict was called 'the war to end all wars'?	*World War I*
4	Who was the River Amazon named after?	*The Amazons (Greek women warriors)*
5	What is the name of Beethoven's only opera?	Fidelio
6	What was the Christian name of Jesse James's brother?	*Frank*
7	Which British football team was nearly wiped out by a plane crash at Munich in 1958?	*Manchester United*
8	How many symphonies did Haydn write: 14, 34 or 104?	*104*
9	Of which country was Antonio Salazar once dictator?	*Portugal*
10	What name was given to the first Spanish invaders of Central and South America?	*Conquistadors*
11	In which century was the first pendulum clock built: 15th, 16th or 17th?	*17th*
12	Which world statesman was once imprisoned on Robben Island off the African coast?	*Nelson Mandela*
13	From which country did the USA buy Alaska in 1867?	*Russia*
14	Where was Captain Cook murdered?	*Hawaii*
15	What is the highest award for bravery in the British Army?	*The Victoria Cross*

Quiz 135
Question 10

Quiz 135
Question 14

Quiz 135
Question 7

Quiz 137 Level 4

	Questions	Answers
1	Which Native American people defeated Custer at the Little Big Horn?	*Sioux*
2	Who led the team which reached the South Pole second?	*R.F. Scott*
3	What was the last battle fought by Horatio Nelson?	*Trafalgar*
4	Who did Britain fight in the Opium War of 1839?	*The Chinese*
5	Which emperor announced in 1946 that he was no longer a god?	*Hirohito of Japan*
6	Who wrote *The Lord of the Flies*?	*William Golding*
7	At which siege did Davy Crockett die in 1836?	*The Alamo*
8	Which drink was invented by Dom Perignon?	*Champagne*
9	Which waterfall in Africa was named after a British queen?	*Victoria Falls*
10	Which pair of aviators first flew the Atlantic in 1919?	*John Alcock and Arthur Brown*
11	Who was the first person to split the atom?	*Ernest Rutherford*
12	Which army unit is bigger, a division or a platoon?	*A division*
13	Which major Australian city is named after a British queen?	*Adelaide*
14	On which Japanese city was the second atomic bomb dropped?	*Nagasaki*
15	What nationality were the Brothers Grimm?	*German*

Quiz 138
Question 8

Quiz 138
Question 5

Quiz 138 Level 4

	Questions	Answers
1	What attachment for rifles is also used to quieten car exhausts?	*The silencer*
2	In which country was Emiliano Zapata a freedom fighter?	*Mexico*
3	Of which country was Jan Smuts the prime minister in 1919?	*South Africa*
4	What language, spoken by white South Africans, is derived from Dutch?	*Afrikaans*
5	What was the popular nickname for James Hickock?	*'Wild Bill' Hickock*
6	Which Swiss mountain was first climbed by Edward Whymper in 1865?	*The Matterhorn*
7	In which year was the modern state of Israel founded?	*1948*
8	What instrument did Django Reinhardt play?	*Guitar*
9	What did Elizabeth Fry devote her life to reforming?	*Prisons and asylums*
10	Which European country conquered Brazil?	*Portugal*
11	Who built the first nuclear reactor, in a squash court, in Chicago?	*Enrico Fermi*
12	What did the letters USSR once stand for?	*Union of Soviet Socialist Republics*
13	Who sailed round the world in a boat named *Gipsy Moth*?	*Sir Francis Chichester*
14	Of which country was Bismarck the chancellor between 1871 and 1890?	*Germany*
15	Who invented the electric battery?	*Alessandro Volta*

Quiz 137
Question 5

Quiz 137
Question 1

Quiz 139 Level 4

	Questions	Answers
1	What was destroyed by a volcanic eruption in AD79?	*The city of Pompeii*
2	By what title was bandleader William Basie known?	*Count*
3	In which year did Julius Caesar first land in Britain – 550BC, 55BC or AD55?	*55BC*
4	Which Italian city is the setting for Shakespeare's *Romeo and Juliet*?	*Verona*
5	Which jazz singer was known as Lady Day?	*Billie Holliday*
6	What nationality was the medieval traveller Ibn Battutah?	*Arabian*
7	In which country is the ancient Walloon language spoken?	*Belgium*
8	Which Apache chief died in 1909?	*Geronimo*
9	Who was defeated at Orleans in 1429 by an English army?	*Joan of Arc*
10	How many countries joined the European Community when it was started in 1957?	*Six*
11	In what year was Nelson Mandela released from prison?	*1990*
12	What leather garment was worn by cowboys over their legs?	*Chaps*
13	Who wrote the music now used for 'Land of Hope and Glory'?	*Elgar*
14	Which city had the first underground railway in 1863?	*London*
15	What do the initials RAF stand for?	*Royal Air Force*

Quiz 140
Question 9

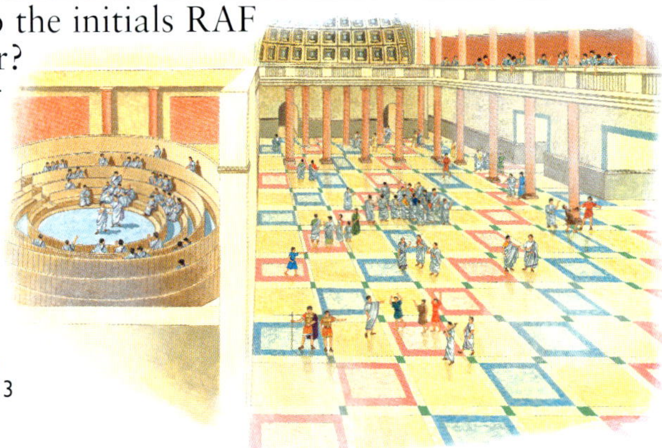

Quiz 140
Question 13

Quiz 140 Level 4

Questions		*Answers*
1	What is the old name for Ethiopia?	*Abyssinia*
2	What computing device did Douglas J. Englebart invent: the hard disk, the joystick or the mouse?	*The mouse*
3	In what band was Michael Hutchence the lead singer and songwriter?	*INXS*
4	Which Sioux leader appeared in Buffalo Bill's Wild West Show?	*Sitting Bull*
5	Who sent the first radio message from England to Australia?	*Guglielmo Marconi*
6	Who was the first European to sail from the Mediterranean to the North Atlantic?	*Pytheas*
7	In which country is the Islamic holy city of Mecca?	*Saudi Arabia*
8	How many crusades were there?	*Eight*
9	Who wrote the play *The Importance of Being Earnest*?	*Oscar Wilde*
10	Which two countries fought out the Hundred Years' War?	*England and France*
11	What important body in Iceland is called the Althing?	*Parliament*
12	Which Celtic queen led a revolt against the Romans?	*Boudicca*
13	Where did Roman senators meet to discuss matters of state?	*The Senate*
14	In what century was the last civil war in Britain?	*The 17th century*
15	What nationality was George Bernard Shaw?	*Irish*

Quiz 139
Question 8

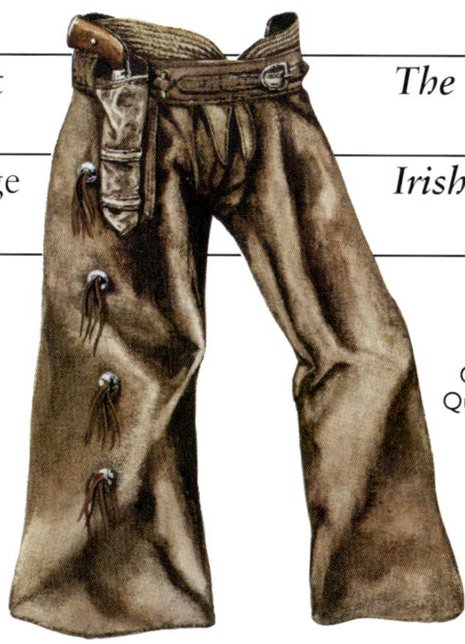

Quiz 139
Question 12

Quiz 141 Level 4

	Questions	Answers
1	In the War of American Independence, which country joined in on America's side in 1779?	*Spain*
2	Which country was Menachem Begin leader of in the 1970s?	*Israel*
3	In which war did Robert E. Lee surrender to Ulysses S. Grant?	*American Civil War*
4	Of which African country was Idi Amin the dictator?	*Uganda*
5	Which hated queen of France was executed in 1793?	*Marie Antoinette*
6	What did Jethro Tull invent in the 18th century?	*The seed drill*
7	Who painted *The Scream*?	*Edvard Munch*
8	Which religion has its centre at the Golden Temple in Amritsar, India?	*Sikhism*
9	Which big country was named by mistake after the Native American word for 'village'?	*Canada*
10	Who were the losing side at the Battle of Blenheim?	*The French*
11	Was Hieronymus Bosch a film star, a rock singer or a painter?	*Painter*
12	What nationality was psychoanalyst Sigmund Freud?	*Austrian*
13	What kind of weapon was a matchlock?	*A firearm ignited by a match*
14	In which Asian country would you find the ruined city of Angkor?	*Cambodia*
15	Which Lady ruled Britain for just nine days?	*Lady Jane Grey*

Quiz 142
Question 6

Quiz 142
Question 12

Quiz 142 Level 4

Questions		Answers
1	What radioactive element was discovered by Pierre and Marie Curie?	*Radium*
2	What African warriors fought in groups called impis?	*Zulus*
3	What was the name of the 'land of milk and honey' where Abraham led the Israelites?	*Canaan*
4	What invention by Elisha Otis in 1854 made it easier to live in skyscrapers?	*The elevator*
5	What kind of animal was the 18th century artist George Stubbs famous for painting?	*The horse*
6	Which Stuart king ruled from 1488 to 1513?	*James IV of Scotland*
7	In which war was the Battle of Antietam (1862)?	*American Civil War*
8	Where, in ancient Greek myth, was the River Styx?	*The Underworld*
9	Who wrote *Kidnapped*?	*Robert Louis Stevenson*
10	Which explorer was set adrift in a small boat by his mutinous crew in 1610?	*Henry Hudson*
11	Which war was ended by the Battle of Yorktown in 1781?	*The American Revolution*
12	What did blacksmith Kirkpatrick Macmillan invent in 1839?	*The world's first pedal-driven bicycle*
13	Where was the Battle of Midway fought in 1942?	*North Pacific*
14	What didn't the British government fund until the 1830s?	*Schools*
15	What was the name of Shakespeare's wife?	*Anne Hathaway*

Quiz 141 Question 12

Quiz 141 Question 6

Quiz 141 Question 8

Quiz 143 Level 4

No.	Questions	Answers
1	Who led North Vietnam in the war against US forces?	*Ho Chi Minh*
2	Which singer was known as 'The Big O'?	*Roy Orbison*
3	Who was the Egyptian god of the underworld?	*Osiris*
4	John Logie Baird is associated with the invention of what machine?	*Television*
5	George Stephenson invented what form of transport?	*The steam locomotive*
6	What kind of ships fought in the Battle of Lepanto in 1571?	*Galleys (oar-driven)*
7	What was the Ancient Roman name for Ireland?	*Hibernia*
8	In which World War II battle did over 100,000 German troops surrender to the Russians?	*Stalingrad*
9	Which city's main art gallery is called the Uffizi?	*Florence*
10	Where do the aboriginals called the Ainu live?	*Japan*
11	Which city's main art gallery is called the Prado?	*Madrid*
12	Who was executed in front of Whitehall Palace in 1649?	*King Charles I*
13	In which Chinese square were more than 1,000 demonstrators killed in 1989?	*Tiananmen*
14	'Lawrence of Arabia' helped Arabs to rebel. Against which country?	*Turkey*
15	What was the name of the Turkish empire which ruled from the 13th century until 1918?	*Ottoman Empire*

Quiz 144 Question 4

Quiz 144 Question 10

Quiz 144 Level 4

	Questions	Answers
1	Which poet said his love was like "a red, red rose"?	*Robert Burns*
2	Who wrote *The Communist Manifesto* with Karl Marx?	*Friedrich Engels*
3	Which branch of the British armed forces was founded by Alfred the Great?	*The navy*
4	Who wrote the novel *Far From the Madding Crowd*?	*Thomas Hardy*
5	Which English king was originally Prince of Orange?	*William III*
6	Which African river did early explorers believe to start in 'The Mountains of the Moon'?	*Nile*
7	What strange tax was abolished in Britain in 1851?	*Tax on windows*
8	Who revolutionized surgery by using carbolic acid as a disinfectant?	*Joseph Lister*
9	Which side won the first Rugby Union World Cup in 1987?	*South Africa*
10	Which war was won and lost at the Battle of Naseby in 1645?	*English Civil War*
11	Nicholas Breakspear was the only English one. What?	*Pope*
12	What breakthrough in photography was pioneered by James Clerk Maxwell?	*Colour photography*
13	Which side won the first Cricket World Cup in 1975?	*West Indies*
14	Which war is the setting for *Catch-22*?	*World War II*
15	When were the last hangings in Britain?	*1964*

Quiz 143 Question 4

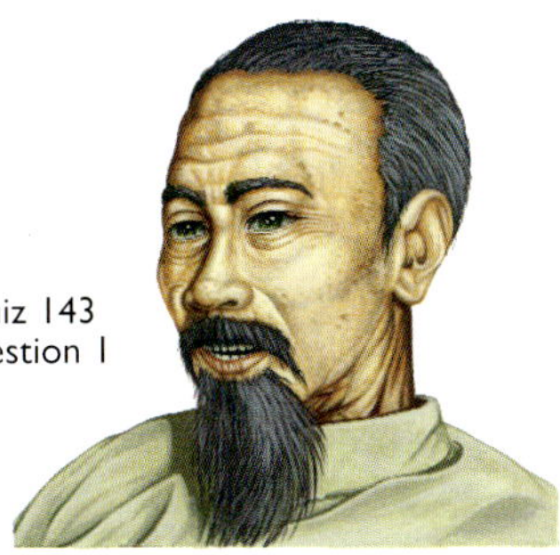
Quiz 143 Question 1

Quiz 143 Question 3

Quiz 145 Level 4

	Questions	Answers
1	Was David Garrick an inventor, an actor or an explorer?	*Actor*
2	In which city did the Triad gangs begin operating?	*Hong Kong*
3	Was Frank Lloyd Wright a painter, an architect, or a composer?	*Architect*
4	Which Swedish chemist invented the explosive, gelignite?	*Alfred Nobel*
5	Which opera singer had a special dessert named after her?	*Nellie Melba*
6	What scandal forced Richard Nixon to resign as US president?	*Watergate*
7	Which 'Great' leader created a vast empire from Greece to India in the period 336-323BC?	*Alexander the Great*
8	What kind of bombs were Fat Man and Big Boy?	*Atomic bombs*
9	Why did Australian explorers die before completing their great journey in 1861?	*Starvation*
10	Who was Britain's prime minister before Winston Churchill in 1940?	*Neville Chamberlain*
11	Who stole fire from Mount Olympus, according to the Greek myths?	*Prometheus*
12	Who built three bridges over the River Severn and two aqueducts?	*Thomas Telford*
13	Which guerrilla army fought against the British in Kenya during the 1950s?	*The Mau-Mau*
14	Which famous monument was sold by auction in 1915 for £6,600?	*Stonehenge*
15	Who, with Wellington, led the victorious armies at Waterloo in 1815?	*Blücher*

Quiz 146
Question 8

Quiz 146
Question 14

Quiz 146 Level 4

	Questions	Answers
1	Which European country was unified in 1861?	*Italy*
2	Which instrument is associated with Andrés Segovia?	*The Spanish guitar*
3	Who sailed in the *Beagle*?	*Charles Darwin*
4	In the Bible, whose wife was turned into a pillar of salt?	*Lot*
5	Who was Conservative leader before Margaret Thatcher?	*Edward Heath*
6	Which US president defeated the British in battle at New Orleans?	*Andrew Jackson*
7	In the stories by P.G. Wodehouse, who is Bertie Wooster's manservant?	*Jeeves*
8	Where did Robert Peary claim to have reached first in 1909?	*The North Pole*
9	Who sits on the woolsack in the House of Lords?	*The Lord Chancellor*
10	How many arrows could a longbowman shoot in a minute?	*Up to 15*
11	How many years did Deng Xiaopeng rule China for?	*Twenty*
12	Which instrument is associated with Charlie Parker?	*Alto saxophone*
13	How would you have kowtowed to a Chinese emperor?	*Bowed down to the floor in front of him*
14	Which Indian prime minister was assassinated by her own bodyguards in 1984?	*Indira Gandhi*
15	What was the name given to the North's forces in the American Civil War?	*Union*

Quiz 145 Question 7

Quiz 145 Question 14

Quiz 147 Level 4

	Questions	Answers
1	By what name is the religious group 'The Society of Friends' better known?	*The Quakers*
2	Who was the last Russian tsar?	*Nikolaus II*
3	What revolt did Wat Tyler lead in 1381?	*The Peasants' Revolt*
4	Which island's ancient parliament is called the House of Keys?	*The Isle of Man*
5	Which famous pop star was shot dead in New York in 1980?	*John Lennon*
6	Which English king was defeated at Bosworth in 1485?	*Richard III*
7	Which country offered Albert Einstein its presidency in 1948?	*Israel*
8	What names did explorers give to the two branches of the River Nile?	*The White Nile and the Blue Nile*
9	Who discovered how to measure the flow of an electric current?	*André Marie Ampère*
10	By what name is the Mongol ruler Timur the Lame better known?	*Tamerlane*
11	Where was Napoleon exiled after his defeat at Waterloo?	*St Helena*
12	Who won the Six-Day War in 1967?	*Israel*
13	Which instrument did Beethoven write his *Emperor Concerto* for?	*Piano (and orchestra)*
14	What was the largest amphitheatre in Roman times?	*The Colosseum*
15	At which London Underground station did 31 people lose their lives in 1987?	*King's Cross*

Quiz 148
Question 11

Quiz 148 Level 4

	Questions	*Answers*
1	Which composer wrote comic operas with W.S. Gilbert?	*Arthur Sullivan*
2	Which country won the first ever football World Cup in 1930?	*Uruguay*
3	In what year was the Hubble Space telescope launched?	*1990*
4	Who threatened to use biological weapons against Israel during the Gulf War?	*Saddam Hussein*
5	Which king was the first British settlement in America named after?	*James I (Jamestown)*
6	In which city was the liner *Titanic* built?	*Belfast*
7	Which Scots leader defeated the English at Stirling Bridge?	*William Wallace*
8	What depicted the Battle of Hastings in 72 scenes?	*The Bayeaux Tapestry*
9	Which Italian family ruled Florence from the 15th century to the 18th century?	*The Medici family*
10	What was abolished in the British Empire in 1833?	*Slavery*
11	From what ship was the first SOS message broadcast?	*The* Titanic
12	What was the nickname of US General Norman Schwarzkopf during the Gulf War?	*Stormin' Norman*
13	Which French monarch was known as 'the Sun King'?	*Louis XIV*
14	In which German town were the Nazi war leaders put on trial?	*Nuremberg*
15	In which World War I battle, lasting 141 days, did the British and French lose 600,000 men?	*The Somme*

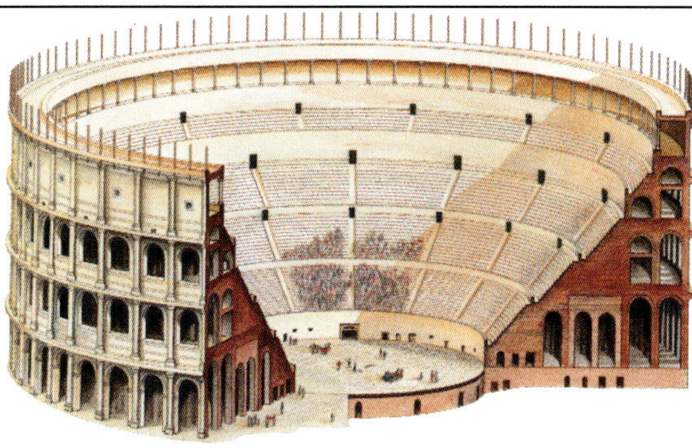

Quiz 147
Question 14

Quiz 149 Level 4

Questions		*Answers*
1	In 1936, a march protesting about unemployment set off from which northern town?	*Jarrow*
2	What nationality was King Canute of England?	*Danish*
3	What is a buckler?	*A small shield*
4	What kind of rope did cowboys use to catch wild horses?	*Lasso*
5	What nationality was Henry the Navigator?	*Portuguese*
6	Who was the first person, in 1875, to swim the English Channel?	*Matthew Webb*
7	Which famous Indian leader was known as The Mahatma, meaning 'great soul'?	*Gandhi*
8	Between which two towns did the first passenger steam trains run?	*Liverpool and Manchester*
9	For which sport was Franz Klammer famous?	*Skiing*
10	What was the name of the first atomic-powered submarine?	Nautilus
11	Who was the only American president to serve three consecutive terms in office?	*Franklin D. Roosevelt*
12	What kind of firearm was invented by Hiram S.Maxim in 1884?	*The automatic machine gun*
13	What invention did Louis Daguerre help to develop in the 1820s?	*Photography*
14	Who was the first monarch of the House of Windsor?	*George V*
15	What party was formed by Anton Drexler in 1919?	*The Nazi Party*

Quiz 150 Question 6

Quiz 150 Question 2

Quiz 150 Level 4

Questions		*Answers*
1	In what year was Pope John Paul II elected?	*1978*
2	What was the name of the US space station?	Skylab
3	Which Canadian ice-hockey player was known as 'The Great One'?	*Wayne Gretzky*
4	Where were the 'murder holes' in a medieval castle?	*Above the gateway passage*
5	What religion was introduced into Japan in 552?	*Buddhism*
6	What African ape was first seen by a Western explorer in the 1850s?	*The gorilla*
7	What household appliance was invented by Sir John Harington in 1596?	*The flushing lavatory*
8	In what year did Prince Charles and Princess Diana agree a divorce?	*1996*
9	What type of machine were the *R101* and the *Hindenberg*, both built in the 1930s?	*Passenger airships*
10	Which British commander won the Battle of Plassey in 1757?	*Robert Clive*
11	Was the Battle of Sluys (1340) fought on land or at sea?	*At sea*
12	Who led the first recorded expedition inside the Antarctic Circle?	*James Cook*
13	What famous building in India was completed in 1643?	*Taj Mahal*
14	On which island did Eric the Red establish the first Viking colony?	*Greenland*
15	Who came to the throne when Queen Victoria died?	*Edward VII*

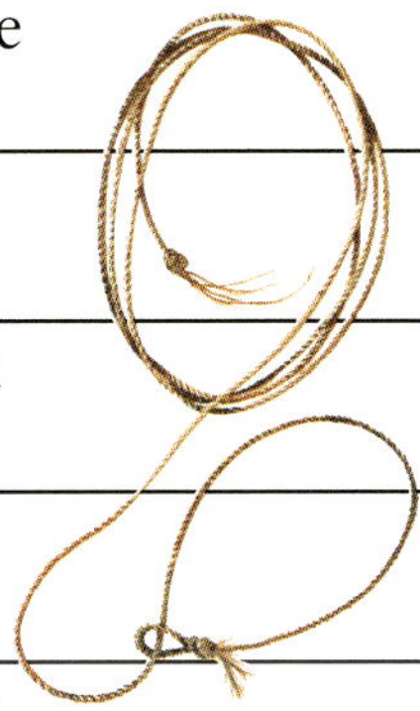

Quiz 149 Question 4

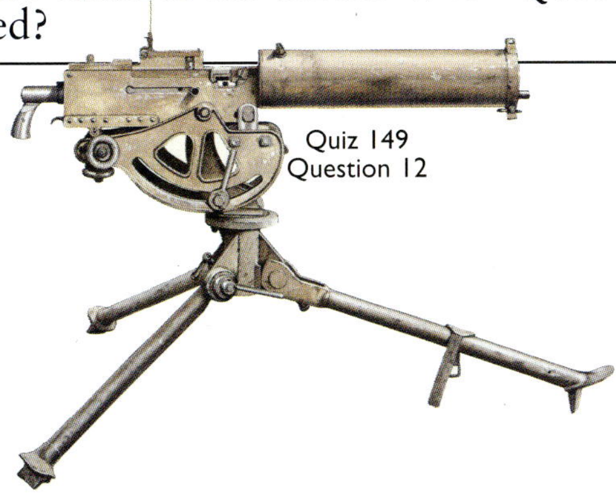

Quiz 149 Question 12

Quiz 149 Question 3

Quiz 151 Level 4

	Questions	Answers
1	Who was assassinated in 1968 by James Earl Ray?	*Martin Luther King*
2	What did the Hudson Bay Company, set up in 1680, trade in?	*Furs*
3	Which country is the setting for the film *Saving Private Ryan*?	*France*
4	Who was the first criminal captured by the use of radio?	*The murderer H.H. Crippen*
5	Which part of Germany was ruled by Frederick the Great?	*Prussia*
6	Ferdinand Magellan was the first man to sail around the world: true or false?	*False: he died on the voyage*
7	By what name is East Pakistan now known?	*Bangladesh*
8	Which royal house did both Edward I and Richard II belong to?	*House of Plantagenet*
9	What is the modern term for a Roman soldier's 'pilum'?	*Spear*
10	Which 17th century scientist proved that blood circulates through the body?	*William Harvey*
11	In which century did Marco Polo visit China?	*13th century*
12	What important document was signed at Runnymede in the 13th century?	*Magna Carta*
13	In which century was the first photograph taken?	*The 19th century*
14	Who wrote the piano music *Clare de Lune?*	*Claude Debussy*
15	Who flew the Atlantic in the *Spirit of St Louis*?	*Charles Lindbergh*

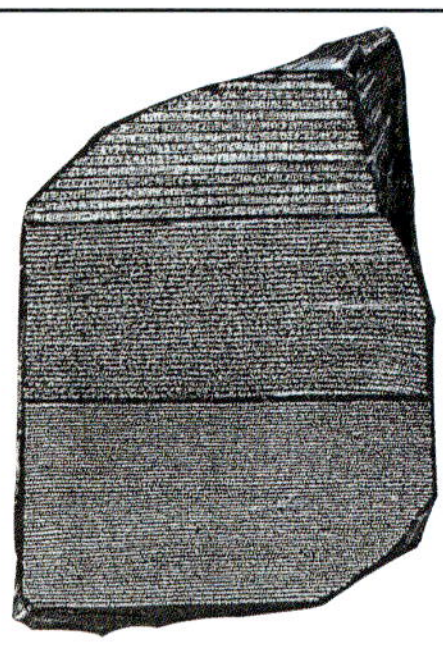

Quiz 152 Question 4

Quiz 152 Question 3

Quiz 152 Level 4

Questions		*Answers*
1	Which city did Marco Polo start his Chinese journey from?	*Venice*
2	What famous newspaper was published for the first time in 1785?	The Times
3	Who were the first settlers to explore the Rockies?	*Trappers*
4	What stone gave the code to hieroglyphic writing?	*The Rosetta Stone*
5	Which country did Bernardo O'Higgins help to liberate in 1818?	*Chile*
6	What was the Praetorian Guard designed to protect?	*Rome and its emperor*
7	Who found the first northerly route from the Atlantic to the Pacific?	*Roald Amundsen*
8	How many children were born to Queen Victoria?	*Seven*
9	What kind of creature is carved into the hillside at Uffington, on the Berkshire Downs?	*A horse*
10	Which painting by Picasso commemorates the bombing of a Spanish village in 1937?	*Guernica*
11	Which space shuttle exploded in flight, killing all crew members?	Challenger
12	What did the Lumière brothers invent?	*The cinematograph*
13	Who was the first wife of King Henry VIII?	*Catherine of Aragon*
14	What type of weapon was a Brown Bess?	*A type of musket*
15	With what kind of surgery is Christiaan Barnard associated?	*Heart transplants*

Quiz 151
Question 12

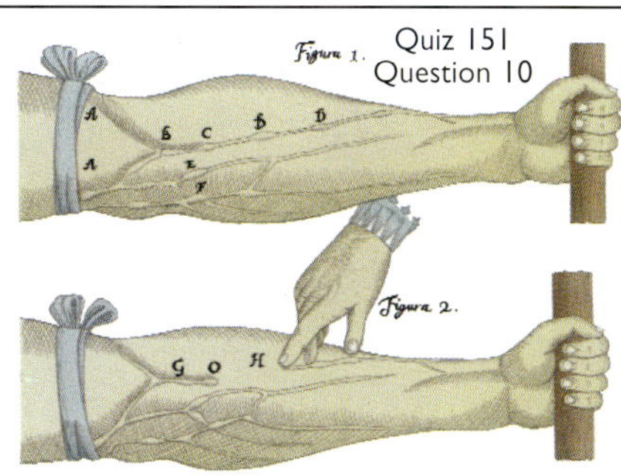

Quiz 151
Question 10